I0168345

A Volunteer Poilu

Henry Sheahan

Contents

A VOLUNTEER POILU

BY

Henry Sheahan

A VOLUNTEER POILU
by Henry Sheahan

To Professor Charles Townsend Copeland of Harvard University
Dear Copey,

At Verdun I thought of you, and the friendly hearth of Hollis 15 seemed very far away from the deserted, snow-swept streets of the tragic city. Then suddenly I remembered how you had encouraged me and many others to go over and help in any way that we could; I remembered your keen understanding of the Epic, and the deep sympathy with human beings which you taught those whose privilege it was to be your pupils. And so you did not seem so far away after all, but closer to the heart of the war than any other friend I had.

I dedicate this book to you with grateful affection after many years of friendship.

Henry
Topsfield, September, 1916

Preface

I have ventured to call this book A Volunteer Poilu principally because we were known to the soldiers of the Bois-le-Pretre as "les Poilus Americains." Then, too, it was my ambition to do for my comrades, the French private soldiers, what other books have done for the soldiers of other armies. The title chosen, however, was more than complimentary; it was but just. In recognition of the work of the

Section during the summer, it was, in October, 1915, formally adopted into the French army; a French officer became its administrative head, and the drivers were given the same papers, pay, and discipline as their French comrades.

I wish to thank many of my old friends of Section II, who have aided me in the writing of this book.

HENRY SHEAHAN

Chapter I
The Rochambeau S'en Va-t-en Guerre

Moored alongside a great two-storied pier, with her bow to the land, the cargo and passenger boat, Rochambeau, of the Compagnie Generale was being loaded with American supplies for the France of the Great War. A hot August sun struck spots and ripples of glancing radiance from the viscous, oily surface of the foul basin in which she lay inert; the air was full of sounds, the wheezing of engines, the rattling of cog-checks, and the rumble of wheels and hoofs which swept, in sultry puffs of noise and odor, from the pavements on the land. Falling from the exhausts, a round, silvery-white cascade poured into the dark lane between the wharf and the deck, and sounded a monotonous, roaring underchord to the intermingled dins. At the sun-bathed bow, a derrick gang lowered bags of flour into the open well of the hold; there were commands in French, a chugging, and a hissing of steam, and a giant's clutch of dusty, hundred-kilo flour-bags from Duluth would swing from the wharf to the Rochambeau, sink, and disappear. In some way the unfamiliar language, and the sight of the thickset, French sailor-men, so evidently all of one race, made the Rochambeau, moored in the shadow of the sky-scrapers, seem mysteriously alien. But among the workers in the hold, who could be seen when they stood on the floor of the open hatchway, was a young, red-headed, American longshoreman clad in the trousers part of a suit of brown-check overalls; sweat and grime had befouled his rather foolish, freckled face, and every time that a bunch of flour-bags tumbled to the floor of the well, he would cry to an invisible somebody--"More dynamite, Joe, more dynamite!"

Walking side by side, like ushers in a wedding procession, two of the ship's officers made interminable rounds of the deck. Now and then they stopped and looked over the rail at the loading operations, and once in low tones they discussed the day's communique. "Pas grand' chose" (nothing of importance), said he whom I took to be the elder, a bearded, seafaring kind of man. "We have occupied a crater in the Argonne, and driven back a German patrol (une patrouille Boche) in the region of Nomeny." The younger, blond, pale, with a wispy yellow mustache, listened casually, his eyes fixed on the turbulence below. The derrick gang were now stowing away clusters of great wooden boxes marked the Something Arms Company. "My brother says that American bullets are filled with powder of a very good quality" (d'une tres bonne qualite), remarked the latter. "By the way, how is your brother?" asked the bearded man. "Very much better," answered the other; "the last fragment (eclat) was taken out of his thigh just before we left Bordeaux." They continued their walk, and three little French boys wearing English sailor hats took their places at the rail.

As the afternoon advanced, a yellow summer sun, sinking to a level with the upper fringes of the city haze, gave a signal for farewells; and little groups retired to quieter corners for good-byes. There was a good deal of worrying about submarines; one heard fragments of conversations--"They never trouble the Bordeaux route"--"Absolutely safe, je t'assure"; and in the accents of Iowa the commanding advice, "Now, don't worry!" "Good-bye, Jim! Good-bye, Maggie!" cried a rotund, snappy American drummer, and was answered with cheery, honest wishes for "the success of his business." Two young Americans with the same identical oddity of gait walked to and fro, and a little black Frenchman, with a frightful star-shaped scar at the corner of his mouth, paraded lonelily. A middle-aged French woman, rouged and dyed back to the thirties, and standing in a nimbus of perfume, wept at the going of a younger woman, and ruined an elaborate make-up with grotesque traceries of tears. "Give him my love," she sobbed; "tell him that the business is doing splendidly and that he is not to buy any of Lafitte's laces next time he goes to Paris en permission." A little later, the Rochambeau, with slow majesty, backed into the channel, and turned her bow to the east.

The chief interest of the great majority of her passengers was commercial; there were American drummers keen to line their pockets with European profits; there were French commis voyageurs who had been selling articles of French manufacture which had formerly been made by the Germans; there were half-official persons who had been on missions to American ammunition works; and there was a diplomat or two. From the sample trunks on board you could have taken any-thing from a pair of boots to a time fuse. Altogether, an interesting lot. Palandeau, a middle-aged Frenchman with a domed, bald forehead like Socrates or Verlaine, had been in America selling eau-de-cologne.

"Then you are getting out something new?" I asked.

"Yes, and no," he answered. "Our product is the old-fashioned eau-de-cologne water with the name 'Farina' on it."

"But in America we associate eau-de-cologne with the Germans," said I. "Doesn't the bottle say 'Johann Maria Farina'? Surely the form of the name is German."

"But that was not his name, monsieur; he was a Frenchman, and called himself 'Jean Marie.' Yes, really, the Germans stole the manufacture from the French. Con-sider the name of the article, 'eau-de-cologne,' is not that French?"

"Yes," I admitted.

"Alors," said Palandeau; "the blocus has simply given us the power to reclaim trade opportunities justly ours. Therefore we have printed a new label telling the truth about Farina, and the Boche 'Johann Maria' is 'kapout.'"

"Do you sell much of it?"

"Quantities! Our product is superior to the Boche article, and has the glamour of an importation. I await the contest without uneasiness."

"What contest?"

"When Jean Marie meets Johann Maria--apres la guerre," said Palandeau with a twinkle in his eye.

In the deck chair next to mine sat a dark, powerfully built young Iowan with the intensely masculine head of a mediaeval soldier. There was a bit of curl to the dark-brown hair which swept his broad, low forehead, his brown eyes were devoid of fear or imagination, his jaw was set, and the big, aggressive head rested on a short, muscular neck. He had been a salesman of machine tools till the "selling end" came to a standstill.

"But didn't the munitions traffic boom the machine-tool industry?" I asked.

"Sure it did. You ought to have seen what people will do to get a lathe. You know about all that you need to make shells is a machine lathe. You can't get a lathe in America for love or money--for anything"--he made a swift, complete gesture--"all making shells. There isn't a junk factory in America that hasn't been pawed over by guys looking for lathes--and my God! what prices! Knew a bird named Taylor who used to make water pipes in Utica, New York--had a stinking little lathe he paid two hundred dollars for, and sold it last year for two thousand. My firm had so many orders for months ahead that it didn't pay them to have salesmen--so they offered us jobs inside; but, God, I can't stand indoor work, so I thought I'd come over here and get into the war. I used to be in the State Cavalry. You ought to have seen how sore all those Iowa Germans were on me for going," he laughed. "Had a hell of row with a guy named Schultz."

Limping slightly, an enormous, grizzled man approached us and sat down by the side of the ex-machinist. Possibly a yellow-gray suit, cut in the bathrobe American style, made him look larger than he was, and though heavily built and stout, there was something about him which suggested ill health. One might have thought him a prosperous American business man on his way to Baden-Baden. He had a big nose, big mouth, a hard eye, and big, freckled hands which he nervously opened and closed.

"See that feller over there?" He pointed to a spectacled individual who seemed lost in melancholy speculation at the rail--"Says he's a Belgian lieutenant. Been over here trying to get cloth. Says he can't get it, the firms over here haven't got the colors. Just think of it, there isn't a pound of Bernheim's blue in the whole country!"

"I thought we were beginning to make dyes of our own," said the Iowan.

"Oh, yes, but we haven't got the hang of it yet. The product is pretty poor. Most of the people who need dyes are afraid to use the American colors, but they've got to take what they can get. Friend of mine, Lon Seeger, of Seeger, Seeger & Hall, the carpet people in Hackensack, had twenty-five thousand dollars' worth of mats spoiled on him last week by using home dyes."

The Belgian lieutenant, still standing by the rail, was talking with another passenger, and some fragments of the conversation drifted to our ears. I caught the words--"My sister--quite unexpected--barely escaped--no doubt of it--I myself saw near Malines--perfectly dreadful--tout-a-fait terrible."

"Twenty-five thousand dollars' worth of mats all spoiled, colors ran, didn't set, no good. This war is raising the devil with the United States textiles. Maybe the Germans won't get a glad hand when they come back. We hear that they're going to flood the market with good, low-priced dyes so as to bust up the new American plants. Haven't you heard them hollerin' for tariff protection? I'm going over to look up a new green dye the French are getting out. We hear it's pretty good stuff. What are you boys doing, looking for contracts?"

The Iowan replied that he hoped to get into an English cavalry regiment, and I mentioned the corps I had joined.

"Well, don't get killed," exclaimed the dye-stuffs agent paternally, and settled down in his chair for a nap.

It was the third day out; the ocean was still the salty green color of the American waters, and big, oily, unrippled waves were rising and falling under the August sun. From the rail I saw coming toward us over the edge of the earth, a small tramp steamer marked with two white blotches which, as the vessel neared, resolved themselves into painted reproductions of the Swedish flag. Thus passed the Thorvald, carrying a mark of the war across the lonely seas.

"That's a Swedish boat," said a voice at my elbow.

"Yes," I replied.

A boy about eighteen or nineteen, with a fine, clear complexion, a downy face, yellow hair, and blue eyes, was standing beside me. There was something psychologically wrong with his face; it had that look in it which makes you want to see if you still have your purse.

"We see that flag pretty often out in Minnesota," he continued.

"What's your name?" I asked.

"Oscar Petersen," he answered.

"Going over to enlist?" I hazarded.

"You bet," he replied--and an instant later--"Are you?"

I told him of my intention. Possibly because we were in for the same kind of experience he later became communicative. He had run away from home at the age of fourteen, spent his sixteenth year in a reform school, and the rest of his time as a kind of gangster in Chicago. I can't imagine a more useless existence than the one he revealed. At length he "got sick of the crowd and got the bug to go to war," as he expressed it, and wrote to his people to tell them he was starting, but received no answer. "My father was a Bible cuss," he remarked cheerfully,--"never got over my swiping the minister's watch."

A Chicago paper had printed his picture and a "story" about his going to enlist in the Foreign Legion--"popular young man very well known in the--th ward," said the article. He showed me, too, an extraordinary letter he had received via the newspaper, a letter written in pencil on the cheapest, shabbiest sheet of ruled note-paper, and enclosing five dollars. "I hope you will try to avenge the Lusitania," it said among other things. The letter was signed by a woman.

"Do you speak French?" I asked.

"Not a word," he replied. "I want to be put with the Americans or the Swedes. I speak good Swedish."

Months later, on furlough, I saw in a hospital at Lyons a college classmate who had served in the Foreign Legion. "Did you know a fellow named Petersen?" I asked.

"Yes, I knew him," answered my friend; "he lifted a fifty-franc note from me and got killed before I could get it back."

"How did it happen?"

"Went through my pockets, I imagine."

"Oh, no, I meant how did he get killed?" "Stray shell sailed in as we were going through a village, and caught him and two of the other boys."

"You must not make your friend talk too much," mumbled an old Sister of Charity rather crossly.

The two young men with the same identical oddity of gait were salesmen of artificial legs, each one a wearer and demonstrator of his wares. The first, from Ohio, had lost his leg in a railroad accident two years before, and the second, a Virginian with a strong accent, had been done for in a motor-car smashup. One morning the man from Ohio gave us a kind of danse macabre on the deck; rolling his trouser leg high above his artificial shin, he walked, leaped, danced, and ran. "Can you beat that?" he asked with pardonable pride. "Think what these will mean to the soldiers." Meanwhile, with slow care, the Virginian explained the ingenious mechanism.

Strange tatters of conversation rose from the deck. "Poor child, she lost her husband at the beginning of the war"--"Third shipment of hosses"--"I was talking with a feller from the Atlas Steel Company"--"Edouard is somewhere near Arras"; there were disputes about the outcome of the war, and arguments over profits. A voluble French woman, whose husband was a pastry cook in a New York hotel before he joined the forces, told me how she had wandered from one war movie to another hoping to catch a glimpse of her husband, and had finally seen "some one who resembled him strongly" on the screen in Harlem. She had a picture of him, a thin, moody fellow with great, saber whiskers like Rostand's and a high, narrow forehead curving in on the sides between the eyebrows and the hair. "He is a Chasseur alpin," she said with a good deal of pride, "and they are holding his place for him at the hotel. He was wounded last month in the shoulder. I am going to the hospital at Lyons to see him." The day's sunset was at its end, and a great mass of black clouds surged over the eastern horizon, turning the seas ahead to a leaden somberness that lowered in menacing contrast to the golden streaks of dying day. The air freshened, salvos of rain fell hissing into the dark waters, and violet cords of lightning leaped between sea and sky. Echoing thunder rolled long through unseen abysses. In the deserted salon I found the young Frenchman with the star-shaped scar reading an old copy of "La Revue." He had been an officer in the Chasseurs-a-pied until a fearful wound had incapacitated him for further service, and had then joined the staff of a great, conservative Parisian weekly. The man was a disciple of Ernest Psichari, the soldier mystic who died so superbly at Charleroi in the dreadful days before the Marne. From him I learned something of the French conception of the idea of war. It was not uninteresting to compare the French point of view with the German, and we talked late into the night while the ship was plunging through the storm. An article in the review, "La Psychologie des Barbares," was the starting-point of our conversation.

"You must remember that the word 'barbarian' which we apply to the Germans, is understood by the French intellectually," said he. "Not only do German atrocities seem barbarous, but their thought also. Consider the respective national conceptions of the idea of war. To the Germans, war is an end in itself, and in itself and in all its effects perfect and good. To the French mind, this conception of war is barbaric, for war is not good in itself and may be fatal to both victor and vanquished." (He spoke a beautiful, lucid French with a sort of military preciseness.)

"It was Ernest Psichari who revealed to us the raison d'etre of arms in modern life, and taught us the meaning of war. To him, war was no savage ruee, but the discipline of history for which every nation must be prepared, a terrible discipline neither to be sought, nor rejected when proffered. Thus the Boches, once their illusion of the glory of war is smashed, have nothing to fall back on, but the French point of view is stable and makes for a good morale. Psichari was the intellectual leader of that movement for the regeneration of the army which has saved France. When the doctrines of pacificism began to be preached in France, and cries of 'A bas l'armee' were heard in the streets, Psichari showed that the army was the only institution left in our industrialized world with the old ideals and the power to teach them. Quand on a tout dit, the military ideals of honor, duty, and sacrifice of one's all for the common good are the fundamentals of. character. Psichari turned this generation from a generation of dreamers to a generation of soldiers, knowing why they were soldiers, glad to be soldiers. The army saved the morale of France when the Church had lost its hold, and the public schools had been delivered to the creatures of sentimental doctrinaire government. Was it not a pity that Psichari should have died so young?"

"Did you know him?" I asked.

"Yes; I saw something of him in Africa. The mystery of the East had profoundly stirred him. He was a dark, serious fellow with something of the profile of his grandfather, Ernest Renan. At Charleroi, after an heroic stand, he and every man of his squad died beside the guns they served."

Long after, at the Bois-le-Pretre, I went to the trenches to get a young sergeant. His friends had with clumsy kindness gathered together his little belongings and put them in the ambulance. "As tu trouve mon livre?" (Have you found my book?) he asked anxiously, and they tossed beside the stretcher a trench-mired copy of Psichari's "L'Appel des Armes."

One morning, just at dawn, we drew near a low, sandy coast, and anchored at the mouth of the great estuary of the Gironde. A spindly lighthouse was flashing, seeming more to reflect the sunlight from outside than to be burning within, and a current the color of coffee and cream with a dash of vermilion in it, went by us mottled with patches of floating mud. From the deck one had an extraordinary view, a ten-mile sweep of the strangely colored water, the hemisphere of the heavens all of one greenish-blue tint, and a narrow strip of nondescript, sandy coast suspended somehow between the strange sea and unlovely sky. At noon, the Rochambeau began at a good speed her journey up the river, passing tile-roofed villages and towns built of pumice-gray stone, and great flat islands covered with acres upon acres of leafy, bunchy vines. There was a scurry to the rail; some one cried, "Voila des Boches," and I saw working in a vineyard half a dozen men in gray-green German regimentals. A poilu in a red cap was standing nonchalantly beside them. As the Rochambeau, following the channel, drew incredibly close to the bank, the Germans leaned on their hoes and watched us pass, all save one, who continued to hoe industriously round the roots of the vines, ignoring us with a Roman's disdain. "Comme ils sont laids" (How ugly they are), said a voice. There was no surprise in the tone, which expressed the expected confirmation of a past judgment. It was the pastry cook's voluble wife who had spoken. The land through which we were passing, up to that time simply the pleasant countryside of the Bordelais, turned in an instant to the France of the Great War.

Late in the afternoon, the river, slowly narrowing, turned a great bend, and the spires of Bordeaux, violet-gray in the smoky rose of early twilight, were seen just ahead. A broad, paved, dirty avenue, with the river on one side and a row of shabby houses on the other, led from the docks to the city, and down this street, marching with Oriental dignity, came a troop of Arabs. There was a picture of a fat sous-officier leading, of brown-white rags and mantles waving in the breeze blowing from the harbor, of lean, muscular, black-brown legs, and dark, impassive faces. "Algerian recruits," said an officer of the boat. It was a first glimpse at the universality of the war; it held one's mind to realize that while some were quitting their Devon crofts, others were leaving behind them the ancestral well at the edges of the ancient desert. A faint squeaking of strange pipes floated on the twilight air.

There came an official examination of our papers, done in a businesslike way, the usual rumpus of the customs, and we were free to land in France. That evening a friend and I had dinner in a great cafe opening on the principal square in Bordeaux, and tried to analyze the difference between the Bordeaux of the past and the Bordeaux of the war. The ornate restaurant, done in a kind of Paris Exhibition style, and decorated with ceiling frescoes of rosy, naked Olympians floating in golden mists and sapphire skies, was full of movement and light, crowds passed by on the sidewalks, there were sounds--laughter.

"Looks just the same to me," said my friend, an American journalist who had been there in 1912. "Of course there are more soldiers. Outside of that, and a lack of taxicabs and motorcars, the town has not changed."

But there was a difference, and a great difference. There was a terrible absence of youth. Not that youth was entirely absent from the tables and the trottoirs; it was visible, putty-faced and unhealthy-looking, afraid to meet the gaze of a man in uniform, the pitiable jeunesse that could not pass the physical examination of the army. Most of the other young men who bent over the tables talking, or leaned back on a divan to smoke cigarettes, were strangers, and I saw many who were unquestionably Roumanians or Greeks. A little apart, at a corner table, a father and mother were dining with a boy in a uniform much too large for him;--I fancied from the cut of his clothes that he belonged to a young squad still under instruction in the garrisons, and that he was enjoying a night off with his family. Screened from the rest by a clothes rack, a larky young lieutenant was discreetly conversing with a "daughter of joy," and an elderly English officer, severely proper and correct, was reading "Punch" and sipping red wine in Britannic isolation. Across the street an immense poster announced, "Conference in aid of the Belgian Red Cross--the German Outrages in Louvain, Malines, and Liege--illustrated."

We finished our dinner, which was good and not costly, and started to walk to our hotel. Hardly had we turned the corner of the Place, when the life of Bordeaux went out like a torch extinguished by the wind. It was still early in the evening, there was a sound of an orchestra somewhere behind, yet ahead of us, lonely and still, with its shops closed and its sidewalks deserted, was one of the greater streets of Bordeaux. Through the drawn curtains of second stories over little groceries and baker-shops shone the yellow light of lamps. What had happened to the Jean, Paul, and Pierre of this dark street since the war began? What tragedies of sorrow and loneliness might these silent windows not conceal? And every French city is much the same; one notices in them all the subtle lack of youth, and the animation of the great squares in contrast to the somber loneliness of streets and quarters which once were alive and gay. At the Place de l'Opera in Paris, the whirlpool of Parisian life is still turning, but the great streets leading away from the Place de l'Etoile are quiet. Young and old, laborer and shopkeeper, boulevardier and apache are far away holding the tragic lines.

The next morning at the station, I had my first glimpse of that mighty organization which surrounds the militaire. There was a special entrance for soldiers and a special exit for soldiers, and at both of these a long file of blue-clad poilus waited for the countersigning of their furlough slips and military tickets. The mud of the trenches still stained the bottom edges of their overcoats, and their steel helmets were dented and dull. There was something fine about the faces collectively; there was a certain look of tried endurance and perils bravely borne. I heard those on furlough telling the names of their home villages to the officer in charge,--pleasant old names, Saint-Pierre aux Vignes, La Tour du Roi.

A big, obese, middle-aged civilian dressed in a hideous greenish suit, and wearing a pancake cap, sat opposite me in the compartment I had chosen. There was a hard, unfriendly look in his large, fat-encircled eyes, a big mustache curved straight out over his lips, and the short finger nails of his square, puffy fingers were deeply rimmed with dirt. He caught sight of me reading a copy of an English weekly, and after staring at me with an interest not entirely free from a certain hostility, retreated behind the pages of the "Matin," and began picking his teeth. Possibly he belonged to that provincial and prejudiced handful to whom England will always be "Perfidious Albion," or else he took me for an English civilian dodging military service. The French press was following the English recruiting campaign very closely, and the system of volunteer service was not without its critics. "Conscription being considered in England" (On discute la conscription en Angleterre), announced the "Matin" discreetly.

It was high noon; the train had arrived at Angouleme, and was taking aboard a crowd of convalescents. On the station platform, their faces relentlessly illumined by the brilliant light, stood about thirty soldiers; a few were leaning on canes, one was without a right arm, some had still the pallor of the sick, others seemed able-bodied and hearty. Every man wore on the bosom of his coat about half a dozen little aluminum medals dangling from bows of tricolor ribbon. "Pour les blesses, s'il vous plait," cried a tall young woman in the costume and blue cape of a Red-Cross nurse as she walked along the platform shaking a tin collection box under the windows of the train.

To our compartment came three of the convalescents. One was a sturdy, farm-hand sort of fellow, with yellow hair and a yellow mustache--the kind of man who might have been a Norman; he wore khaki puttees, brown corduroy trousers, and a jacket which fitted his heavy, vigorous figure rather snugly. Another was a little soul dressed in the "blue horizon" from head to foot, a homely little soul with an egg-shaped head, brown-green eyes, a retreating chin, and irregular teeth. The last, wearing the old tenue, black jacket and red trousers, was a good-looking fellow with rather handsome brown eyes. Comfortably stretched in a corner, the Norman was deftly cutting slices of bread and meat which he offered to his companions. Catching sight of my English paper, all three stared at me with an interest and friendliness that was in psychological contrast to the attitude of the obese civilian.

"Anglais?" asked the Norman.

The civilian watched for my answer.

"Non--Americain," I replied.

"Tiens," they said politely.

"Do you speak English?" asked the homely one.

"Yes," I answered.

The Norman fished a creased dirty letter and a slip of paper from his wallet and handed them to me for inspection.

"I found them in a trench we shared with the English," he explained. "These puttees are English; a soldier gave them to me." He exhibited his legs with a good deal of satisfaction.

I examined the papers that had been given me. The first was a medical prescription for an anti-lice ointment and the second an illiterate letter extremely difficult to decipher, mostly about somebody whom the writer was having trouble to manage, "now that you aren't here." I translated as well as I could for an attentive audience. "Toujours les totos," they cried merrily when I explained the prescription. A spirit of good-fellowship pervaded the compartment, till even the suspicious civilian unbent, and handed round post-card photographs of his two sons who were somewhere en Champagne. Not a one of the three soldiers could have been much over twenty-one, but they were not boys, but men, serious men, tried and disciplined by war. The homely one gave me one of his many medals which he wore "to please the good Sisters"; on one side in an oval of seven stars was the Virgin Mary, and on the other, the determined features of General Joffre.

Just at sundown we crossed the great plain of La Beauce. Distant villages and pointed spires stood silhouetted in violet-black against the burning midsummer sky and darkness was falling upon the sweeping golden plain. We passed hamlet after hamlet closed and shuttered, though the harvests had been gathered and stacked.

There was something very tragic in those deserted, outlying farms. The train began to rattle through the suburbs of Paris. By the window stood the Norman looking out on the winking red and violet lights of the railroad yard. "This Paris?" he asked. "I never expected to see Paris. How the war sets one to traveling!"

Chapter 2
An Unknown Paris in the Night and Rain

It was Sunday morning, the bells were ringing to church, and I was strolling in the gardens of the Tuileries. A bright morning sun was drying the dewy lawns and the wet marble bodies of the gods and athletes, the leaves on the trees were falling, and the French autumn, so slow, so golden, and so melancholy, had begun. At the end of the mighty vista of the Champs Elysees, the Arc de Triomphe rose, brown and vaporous in the exhalations of the quiet city, and an aeroplane was maneuvering over the Place de la Concorde, a moving speck of white and silver in the soft, September blue. From a near-by Punch and Judy show the laughter of little children floated down the garden in outbursts of treble shrillness. "Villain, monster, scoundrel," squeaked a voice. Flopped across the base of the stage, the arms hanging downwards, was a prostrate doll which a fine manikin in a Zouave's uniform belabored with a stick; suddenly it stirred, and, with a comic effect, lifted its puzzled, wooden head to the laughing children. Beneath a little Prussian helmet was the head of William of Germany, caricatured with Parisian skill into a scowling, green fellow with a monster black mustache turned up to his eyes. "Lie down!" cried the Zouave doll imperiously. "Here is a love pat for thee from a French Zouave, my big Boche." And he struck him down again with his staff.

Soldiers walked in the garden,--permissionnaires (men on furlough) out for an airing with their rejoicing families, smart young English subalterns, and rosy-fleshed, golden-haired Flemings of the type that Rubens drew. But neither their presence nor the sight of an occasional mutile (soldier who has lost a limb), pathetically clumsy on his new crutches, quite sent home the presence of the war. The normal life of the city was powerful enough to engulf the disturbance, the theaters were open, there were the same crowds on the boulevards, and the same gossipy spectators in the sidewalk cafes. After a year of war the Parisians were accustomed to soldiers, cripples, and people in mourning. The strongest effect of the war was more subtle of definition, it was a change in the temper of the city. Since the outbreak of the war, the sham Paris that was "Gay Paree" had disappeared, and the real Paris, the Paris of tragic memories and great men, had taken its place. An old Parisian explained the change to me in saying, "Paris has become more French." Deprived of the foreigner, the city adapted itself to a taste more Gallic; faced with the realities of war, it exchanged its artificiality for that sober reasonableness which is the normal attitude of the nation.

At noon I left the garden and strolled down the Champs Elysees to the Porte Maillot. The great salesrooms of the German motor-car dealers had been given by the Government to a number of military charities who had covered the trade signs with swathes and rosettes of their national colors. Under the banner of the Belgians, in the quondam hop of the Mercedes, was an exhibition of leather knickknacks, baskets, and dolls made by the blind and mutilated soldiers. The articles--children's toys for the most part, dwarfs that rolled over and over on a set of parallel bars, Alsatian lasses with flaxen hair, and gay tops--were exposed on a row of tables a few feet back from the window. By the Porte Maillot, some of the iron saw-horses with sharpened points, which had formed part of the barricade built there in the days of the Great Retreat, lay, a villainous, rusty heap, in a grassy ditch of the city wall; a few stumps of the trees that had been then cut down were still visible, and from a railroad tie embedded in the sidewalk hung six links of a massive chain. Through this forgotten flotsam on the great shore of the war, the quiet crowds went in and out of the Maillot entrance to the Bois de Boulogne. There was a sense of order and security in the air. I took a seat on the terrace of a little restaurant. The garcon was a small man in the fifties, inclined to corpulence, with a large head, large, blue-gray eyes, purplish lips, and blue-black hair cut pompadour. As we watched the orderly, Sunday crowds going to the great park, we fell into conversation about the calmness of Paris. "Yes, it is calm," he said; "we are all waiting (nous attendons). We know that the victory will be ours at the finish. But all we can do is to wait. I have two sons at the front." He had struck the keynote. Paris is calmly waiting--waiting for the end of the war, for victory, for the return of her children.

Yet in this great, calm city, with its vaporous browns and slaty blues, and its characteristic acrid smell of gasoline fumes, was another Paris, a terrible Paris, which I was that night to see. Early in the afternoon a dull haze of leaden clouds rose in the southwest. It began to rain.

In a great garret of the hospital, under a high French roof, was the dormitory of the volunteers attached to the Paris Ambulance Section. At night, this great space was lit by only one light, a battered electric reading-lamp standing on a kind of laboratory table in the center of the floor, and window curtains of dark-blue cambric, waving mysteriously in the night wind, were supposed to hide even this glimmer from the eyes of raiding Zeppelins. Looking down, early in the evening, into the great quadrangle of the institution, one saw the windows of the opposite wing veiled with this mysterious blue, and heard all the feverish unrest of a hospital, the steps on the tiled corridors, the running of water in the bathroom taps, the hard clatter of surgical vessels, and sometimes the cry of a patient having a painful wound dressed. But late at night the confused murmur of the battle between life and death had subsided, the lights in the wards were extinguished, and only the candle of the night nurse, seen behind a screen, and the stertorous breathing of the many sleepers, brought back the consciousness of human life. I have often looked into the wards as I returned from night calls to the station where we received the wounded, and been conscious, as I peered silently into that flickering obscurity, of the vague unrest of sleepers, of the various attitudes assumed, the arms outstretched, the upturned throats, and felt, too, in the still room, the mystic presence of the Angel of Pain.

It was late at night, and I stood looking out of my window over the roofs of Neuilly to the great, darkened city just beyond. From somewhere along the tracks of the "Little Belt" railway came a series of piercing shrieks from a locomotive whistle. It was raining hard, drumming on the slate roof of the dormitory, and somewhere below a gutter gurgled foolishly. Far away in the corridor a gleam of yellow light shone from the open door of an isolation room where a nurse was watching by a patient dying of gangrene. Two comrades who had been to the movies at the Gaumont Palace near the Place Clichy began to talk in sibilant whispers of the evening's entertainment, and one of them said, "That war film was a corker; did you spot the big cuss throwing the grenades?" "Yuh, damn good," answered the other pulling his shirt over his head. It was a strange crew that inhabited these quarters; there were idealists, dreamers, men out of work, simple rascals and adventurers of all kinds. To my right slept a big, young Westerner, from some totally unknown college in Idaho, who was a humanitarian enthusiast to the point of imbecility, and to the left a middle-aged rogue who indulged in secret debauches of alcohol and water he cajoled from the hospital orderlies. Yet this obscure and motley community was America's contribution to France. I fell asleep.

"Up, birds!"

The lieutenant of the Paris Section, a mining engineer with a picturesque vocabulary of Nevadan profanity, was standing in his pajama trousers at the head of the room, holding a lantern in his hand. "Up, birds!" he called again. "Call's come in for Lah Chapelle." There were uneasy movements under the blankets, inmates of adjoining beds began to talk to each other, and some lit their bedside candles. The chief went down both sides of the dormitory, flashing his lantern before each bed, ragging the sleepy. "Get up, So-and-So. Well, I must say, Pete, you have a hell of a nerve." There were glimpses of candle flames, bare bodies shivering in the damp cold, and men sitting on beds, winding on their puttees. "Gee! listen to it rain," said somebody. "What time is it?" "Twenty minutes past two." Soon the humming and drumming of the motors in the yard sounded through the roaring of the downpour.

Down in the yard I found Oiler, my orderly, and our little Ford ambulance, number fifty-three. One electric light, of that sickly yellow color universal in France, was burning over the principal entrance to the hospital, just giving us light enough to see our way out of the gates. Down the narrow, dark Boulevard Inkerman we turned, and then out on to a great street which led into the "outer" boulevard of De Batignolles and Clichy. To that darkness with which the city, in fear of raiding aircraft, has hidden itself, was added the continuous, pouring rain. In the light of our lamps, the wet, golden trees of the black, silent boulevards shone strangely, and the illuminated advertising kiosks which we passed, one after the other at the corners of great streets, stood lonely and drenched, in the swift, white touch of our radiance. Black and shiny, the asphalt roadway appeared to go on in a straight line forever and forever.

Neither in residential, suburban Neuilly nor in deserted Montmartre was there a light to be seen, but when we drew into the working quarter of La Chapelle, lights appeared in the windows, as if some toiler of the night was expected home or starting for his labor, and vague forms, battling with the rain or in refuge under the awning of a cafe, were now and then visible. From the end of the great, mean rue de La Chapelle the sounds of the unrest of the railroad yards began to be heard, for this street leads to the freight-houses near the fortifications. Our objective was a great freight station which the Government, some months before, had turned into a receiving-post for the wounded; it lay on the edge of the yard, some distance in from the street, behind a huddle of smaller sheds and outbuildings. To our surprise the rue de La Chapelle was strewn with ambulances rushing from the station, and along two sides of the great yard, where the merchandise trucks had formerly turned in, six or seven hundred more ambulances were waiting. We turned out of the dark, rain-swept city into this hurly-burly of shouts, snorting of engines, clashing of gears, and whining of brakes, illuminated with a thousand intermeshing beams of headlights across whose brilliance the rain fell in sloping, liquid rods. "Quick, a small car this way!" cried some one in an authoritative tone, and number fifty-three ran up an inclined plane into the enormous shed which had been reserved for the loading of the wounded into the ambulances.

We entered a great, high, white-washed, warehouse kind of place, about four hundred feet long by four hundred feet wide, built of wood evidently years before. In the middle of this shed was an open space, and along the walls were rows of ambulances. Brancardiers (stretcher-bearers; from brancard, a stretcher) were loading wounded into these cars, and as soon as one car was filled, it would go out of the hall and another would take its place. There was an infernal din; the place smelled like a stuffy garage, and was full of blue gasoline fumes; and across this hurly-burly, which was increasing every minute, were carried the wounded, often nothing but human bundles of dirty blue cloth and fouled bandages. Every one of these wounded soldiers was saturated with mud, a gray-white mud that clung moistly to their overcoats, or, fully dry, colored every part of the uniform with its powder. One saw men that appeared to have rolled over and over in a puddle bath of this whitish mud, and sometimes there was seen a sinister mixture of blood and mire. There is nothing romantic about a wounded soldier, for his condition brings a special emphasis on our human relation to ordinary meat. Dirty, exhausted, unshaven, smelling of the trenches, of his wounds, and of the antiseptics on his wounds, the soldier comes from the train a sight for which only the great heart of Francis of Assisi could have adequate pity.

Oiler and I went through an opening in a canvas partition into that part of the great shed where the wounded were being unloaded from the trains. In width, this part measured four hundred feet, but in length it ran to eight hundred. In two rows of six each, separated by an aisle about eight feet wide, were twelve little houses, about forty feet square, built of stucco, each one painted a different color. The woodwork of the exterior was displayed through the plaster in the Elizabethan fashion, and the little sheds were clean, solidly built, and solidly roofed. In one of these constructions was the bureau of the staff which assigned the wounded to the hospitals, in another was a fully equipped operating-room, and in the others, rows of stretcher-horses, twenty-five to a side, on which the wounded were laid until a hospital number had been assigned them. A slip, with these hospital numbers on it, the names of the patients, and the color of the little house in which they were to be found, was then given to the chauffeur of an ambulance, who, with this slip in hand and followed by a number of stretcher-bearers, immediately gathered his patients. A specimen slip might run thus--"To Hospital 32, avenue de Iena, Paul Chaubard, red barraque, Jules Adamy, green barraque, and Alphonse Fort, ochre barraque."

To give a French touch to the scene, this great space, rapidly filling with human beings in an appalling state of misery, as the aftermath of the offensive broke on us, was decorated with evergreen trees and shrubs so that the effect was that of an indoor fair or exhibition; you felt as if you might get samples of something at each barraque, as the French termed the little houses. To the side of these there was a platform, and a sunken track running along the wall, and behind, a great open space set with benches for those of the wounded able to walk. Some fifty great, cylindrical braziers, which added a strange bit of rosy, fiery color to the scene, warmed this space. When the wounded had begun to arrive at about midnight, a regiment of Zouaves was at hand to help the regular stretcher-bearers; these Zouaves were all young, "husky" men dressed in the baggy red trousers and short blue jacket of their classic uniform, and their strength was in as much of a contrast to the weakness of those whom they handled as their gay uniform was in contrast to the miry, horizon blue of the combatants. There was something grotesque in seeing two of these powerful fellows carrying to the wagons a dirty blue bundle of a human being.

With a piercing shriek, that cut like a gash through the uproar of the ambulance engines, a sanitary train, the seventh since midnight, came into the station, and so smoothly did it run by, its floors on a level with the main floor, that it seemed an illusion, like a stage train. On the platform stood some Zouaves waiting to unload the passengers, while others cleared the barraques and helped the feeble to the ambulances. There was a steady line of stretchers going out, yet the station was so full that hardly a bit of the vast floor space was unoccupied. One walked down a narrow path between a sea of bandaged bodies. Shouldering what baggage they had, those able to walk plodded in a strange, slow tempo to the waiting automobiles. All by themselves were about a hundred poor, ragged Germans, wounded prisoners, brothers of the French in this terrible fraternity of pain.

About four or five hundred assis (those able to sit up) were waiting on benches at the end of the hall. Huddled round the rosy, flickering braziers, they sat profoundly silent in the storm and din that moved about them, rarely conversing with each other. I imagine that the stupefaction, which is the physiological reaction of an intense emotional and muscular effort, had not yet worn away. There were fine heads here and there. Forgetful of his shattered arm, an old fellow, with the face of Henri Quatre, eagle nose, beard, and all, sat with his head sunken on his chest in mournful contemplation, and a fine-looking, black-haired, dragoon kind of youth with the wildest of eyes clung like grim death to a German helmet. The same expression of resigned fatalism was common to all.

Sometimes the chauffeurs who were waiting for their clients got a chance to talk to one of the soldiers. Eager for news, they clustered round the wounded man, bombarding him with questions.

"Are the Boches retreating?"

"When did it begin?"

"Just where is the attack located?"

"Are things going well for us?"

The soldier, a big young fellow with a tanned face, somewhat pale from the shock of a ripped-up forearm, answered the questions good-naturedly, though the struggle had been on so great a scale that he could only tell about his own hundred feet of trench. Indeed the substance of his information was that there had been a terrible bombardment of the German lines, and then an attack by the French which was still in progress.

"Are we going to break clear through the lines?"

The soldier shrugged his shoulders. "They hope to," he replied.

Just beyond us, in one of the thousand stretchers on the floor, a small bearded man had died. With his left leg and groin swathed in bandages, he lay flat on his back, his mouth open, muddy, dirty, and dead. From time to time the living on each side stole curious, timid glances at him. Then, suddenly, some one noticed the body, and two stretcher-bearers carried it away, and two more brought a living man there in its place.

The turmoil continued to increase. At least a thousand motor-ambulances, mobilized from all over the region of Paris, were now on hand to carry away the human wreckage of the great offensive. Ignorant of the ghastly army at its doors, Paris slept. The rain continued to fall heavily.

"Eh la, comrade."

A soldier in the late thirties, with a pale, refined face, hailed me from his stretcher.

"You speak French?"

I nodded.

"I am going to ask you to do me a favor--write to my wife who is here in Paris, and tell her that I am safe and shall let her know at once what hospital I am sent to. I shall be very grateful."

He let his shoulders sink to the stretcher again and I saw him now and then looking for me in the crowd. Catching my eye, he smiled.

A train full of Algerian troops came puffing into the station, the uproar hardly rising above the general hubbub. The passengers who were able to walk got out first, some limping, some walking firmly with a splendid Eastern dignity. These men were Arabs and Moors from Algeria and Tunisia, who had enlisted in the colonial armies. There was a great diversity of size and racial type among them, some being splendid, big men of the type one imagines Othello to have been, some chunkier and more bullet-headed, and others tall and lean with interesting aquiline features. I fancy that the shorter, rounder-skulled ones were those with a dash of black blood. The uniform, of khaki-colored woolen, consisted of a simple, short-waisted jacket, big baggy trousers, puttees, and a red fez or a steel helmet with the lunar crescent and "R.F." for its device. We heard rumors about their having attacked a village. Advancing in the same curious tempo as the French, they passed to the braziers and the wooden benches. Last of all from the train, holding his bandaged arm against his chest, a native corporal with the features of a desert tribesman advanced with superb, unconscious stateliness. As the Algerians sat round the braziers, their uniforms and brown skins presented a contrast to the pallor of the French in their bedraggled blue, but there was a marked similarity of facial expression. A certain racial odor rose from the Orientals.

My first assignment, two Algerians and two Frenchmen, took me to an ancient Catholic high school which had just been improvised into a hospital for the Oriental troops. It lay, dirty, lonely, and grim, just to one side of a great street on the edge of Paris, and had not been occupied since its seizure by the State. Turning in through an enormous door, lit by a gas globe flaring and flickering in the torrents of rain, we found ourselves in an enormous, dark courtyard, where a half-dozen ambulances were already waiting to discharge their clients. Along one wall there was a flight of steps, and from somewhere beyond the door at the end of this stair shone the faintest glow of yellow light.

It came from the door of a long-disused schoolroom, now turned into the receiving-hall of this strange hospital. The big, high room was lit by one light only, a kerosene hand lamp standing on the teacher's desk, and so smoked was the chimney that the wick gave hardly more light than a candle. There was just enough illumination to see about thirty Algerians sitting at the school desks, their big bodies crammed into the little seats, and to distinguish others lying in stretchers here and there upon the floor. At the teacher's table a little French adjutant with a trim, black mustache and a soldier interpreter were trying to discover the identity of their visitors.

"Number 2215," (numero deux mille deux cent quinze), the officer cried; and the interpreter, leaning over the adjutant's shoulder to read the name, shouted, "Mehemet Ali."

There was no answer, and the Algerians looked round at each other, for all the world like children in a school. It was very curious to see these dark, heavy, wild faces bent over these disused desks.

"Number 2168" (numero deux mille cent soixante huit), cried the adjutant.

"Abdullah Taleb," cried the interpreter.

"Moi," answered a voice from a stretcher in the shadows of the floor.

"Take him to room six," said the adjutant, indicating the speaker to a pair of stretcher-bearers. In the quieter pauses the rain was heard beating on the panes.

There are certain streets in Paris, equally unknown to tourist and Parisian--obscure, narrow, cobble-stoned lanes, lined by walls concealing little orchards and gardens. So provincial is their atmosphere that it would be the easiest thing in the world to believe one's self on the fringe of an old town, just where little bourgeois villas begin to overlook the fields; but to consider one's self just beyond the heart of Paris is almost incredible. Down such a street, in a great garden, lay the institution to which our two Frenchmen were assigned. We had a hard time finding it in the night and rain, but at length, discovering the concierge's bell, we sent a vigorous peal clanging through the darkness. Oiler lifted the canvas flap of the ambulance to see about our patients.

"All right in there, boys?"

"Yes," answered a voice.

"Not cold?"

"Non. Are we at the hospital?"

"Yes; we are trying to wake up the concierge."

There was a sound of a key in a lock, and a small, dark woman opened the door. She was somewhat spinstery in type, her thin, black hair was neatly parted in the middle, and her face was shrewd, but not unkindly.

"Deux blesses (two wounded), madame," said I.

The woman pulled a wire loop inside the door, and a far-off bell tinkled.

"Come in," she said. "The porter will be here immediately."

We stepped into a little room with a kind of English look to it, and a carbon print of the Sistine Madonna on the wall.

"Are they seriously wounded?" she asked.

"I cannot say."

A sound of shuffling, slippered feet was heard, and the porter, a small, beefy, gray-haired man in the fifties, wearing a pair of rubber boots, and a rain-coat over a woolen night-dress, came into the room.

"Two wounded have arrived," said the lady. "You are to help these messieurs get out the stretchers."

The porter looked out of the door at the tail-light of the ambulance, glowing red behind its curtain of rain.

"Mon Dieu, what a deluge!" he exclaimed, and followed us forth. With an "Easy there," and "Lift now," we soon had both of our clients out of the ambulance and indoors. They lay on the floor of the odd, stiff, little room, strange intruders of its primness; the first, a big, heavy, stolid, young peasant with enormous, flat feet, and the second a small, nervous, city lad, with his hair in a bang and bright, uneasy eyes. The mud-stained blue of the uniforms seemed very strange, indeed, beside the Victorian furniture upholstered in worn, cherry-red plush. A middle-aged servant--a big-boned, docile-looking kind of creature, probably the porter's wife--entered, followed by two other women, the last two wearing the same cut of prim black waist and skirt, and the same pattern of white wristlets and collar. We then carried the two soldiers upstairs to a back room, where the old servant had filled a kind of enamel dishpan with soapy water. Very gently and deftly the beefy old porter and his wife took off the fouled, blood-stained uniforms of the two fighting men, and washed their bodies, while she who had opened the door stood by and superintended all. The feverish, bright-eyed fellow seemed to be getting weaker, but the big peasant conversed with the old woman in a low, steady tone, and told her that there had been a big action.

When Oiler and I came downstairs, two little glasses of sherry and a plate of biscuits were hospitably waiting for us. There was something distinctly English in the atmosphere of the room and in the demeanor of the two prim ladies who stood by. It roused my curiosity. Finally one of them said:--

"Are you English, gentlemen?"

"No," we replied; "Americans."

"I thought you might be English," she replied in that language, which she spoke very clearly and fluently. "Both of us have been many years in England. We are French Protestant deaconesses, and this is our home. It is not a hospital. But when the call for more accommodations for the wounded came in, we got ready our two best rooms. The soldiers upstairs are our first visitors."

The old porter came uneasily down the stair. "Mademoiselle Pierre says that the doctor must come at once," he murmured, "the little fellow (le petit) is not doing well."

We thanked the ladies gratefully for the refreshment, for we were cold and soaked to the skin. Then we went out again to the ambulance and the rain. A faint pallor of dawn was just beginning. Later in the morning, I saw a copy of the "Matin" attached to a kiosk; it said something about "Grande Victoire."

Thus did the great offensive in Champagne come to the city of Paris, bringing twenty thousand men a day to the station of La Chapelle. For three days and nights the Americans and all the other ambulance squads drove continuously. It was a terrible phase of the conflict to see, but he who neither sees nor understands it cannot realize the soul of the war. Later, at the trenches, I saw phases of the war that were spiritual, heroic, and close to the divine, but this phase was, in its essence, profoundly animal.

Chapter III
The Great Swathe of the Lines

The time was coming when I was to see the mysterious region whence came the wounded of La Chapelle, and, a militaire myself, share the life of the French soldier. Late one evening in October, I arrived in Nancy and went to a hotel I had known well before the war. An old porter, a man of sixty, with big, bowed shoulders, gray hair, and a florid face almost devoid of expression, carried up my luggage, and as I looked at him, standing in the doorway, a simple figure in his striped black and yellow vest and white apron, I wondered just what effect the war had had on him. Through the open window of the room, seen over the dark silhouette of the roofs of Nancy, shone the glowing red sky and rolling smoke of the vast munition works at Pompey and Frouard.

"You were not here when I came to the hotel two years ago," said I.

"No," he answered; "I have been here only since November, 1914."

"You are a Frenchman? There was a Swiss here, then."

"Yes, indeed, I am Francais, monsieur. The Swiss is now a waiter in a cafe of the Place Stanislas. It is something new to me to be a hotel porter."

"Tiens. What did you do?"

"I drove a coal team, monsieur."

"How, then, did you happen to come here?"

"I used to deliver coal to the hotel. One day I heard that the Swiss had gone to the cafe to take the place of a garcon whose class had just been called out. I was getting sick of carrying the heavy sacks of coal, and being always out of doors, so I applied for the porter's job."

"You are satisfied with the change."

"Oh, yes, indeed, monsieur."

"I suppose you have kinsmen at the front."

"Only my sister's son, monsieur."

"In the active forces?"

"No, he is a reservist. He is a man thirty-five years of age. He was wounded by a shrapnel ball in the groin early in the spring, but is now at the front again."

"What does he do en civil?"

"He is a furniture-maker, monsieur."

He showed no sign of unrest at my catechizing, and plodded off down the green velvet carpet to the landing-stage of the elevator. In the street below a crowd was coming out of the silky white radiance of the lobby of a cinema into the violet rays thrown upon the sidewalk from the illuminated sign over the theater door. There are certain French cities to which the war has brought a real prosperity, and Nancy was then one of them. The thousands of refugees from the frontier villages and the world of military officials and soldier workmen mobilized in the ammunition factories had added to the population till it was actually greater than it had been before the war, and with this new population had come a development of the city's commercial life. The middle class was making money, the rich were getting richer, and Nancy, hardly more than eighteen or nineteen miles from the trenches, forgot its danger till, on the first day of January, 1916, the Germans fired several shells from a giant mortar or a marine piece into the town, one of which scattered the fragments of a big five-story apartment house all over Nancy. And on that afternoon thirty thousand people left the city.

The day on which I was to go across the great swathe of the front to the first-line trenches dawned cool and sunny. I use the word "swathe" purposely, for only by that image can the real meaning of the phrase "the front" be understood. The thick, black line which figures on the war-maps is a great swathe of country running, with a thousand little turns and twists that do not interfere with its general regularity, from the summits of the Vosges to the yellow dunes of the North Sea. The relation of the border of this swathe to the world beyond is the relation of sea to land along an irregular and indented coast. Here an isolated, strategic point, fiercely defended by the Germans, has extended the border of the swathe beyond the usual limits, and villages thirteen and fourteen miles from the actual lines have been pounded to pieces by long-range artillery in the hope of destroying the enemy's communications; there the trenches cross an obscure, level moor upon whose possession nothing particular depends, and the swathe narrows to the villages close by the lines. This swathe, which begins with the French communications, passes the French trenches, leaps "No Man's Land," and continues beyond the German trenches to the German communications, averages about twenty-two miles in width. The territory within this swathe is inhabited by soldiers, ruled by soldiers, worked by soldiers, and organized for war.

Sometimes the transition between civilian life and the life of the swathe is abrupt, as, for instance, at Verdun, where the villages beyond the lines have been emptied of civilian inhabitants to make room for the soldiery; but at other times the change is gradual and the peasants continue to work fields almost in the shadow of the trenches. Since the line of trenches was organized by the Germans only after a series of engagements along the front, during which the battle-line oscillated over a wide territory, the approach to the swathe is often through a region of desolated villages sometimes far removed from the present trenches. Such is the state of affairs in the region of the Marne, the Argonne, and on the southern bank of the Moselle. Moss-overgrown and silent, these villages often stand deserted in the fields at the entrance to the swathe, fit heralds of the desolation that lies beyond.

Imagine, then, the French half of the swathe extending from the edge of the civilian world to the barbed-wire entanglements of No Man's Land. Within this territory, in the trenches, in the artillery positions, in the villages where troops are quartered (and they are quartered in every village of the swathe), and along all the principal turns and corners of the roads, a certain number of shells fall every twenty-four hours, the number of shells per locality increasing as one advances toward the first lines. There are certain disputed regions, that of Verdun in particular, where literally the whole great swathe has been pounded to pieces, till hardly one stone of a village remains on another, and during the recent offensive in the Somme the British are said to have systematically wiped out every village, hamlet, and road behind the German trenches to a depth of eighteen miles. Yet, protected from rifle bullets and the majority of shells by a great wooded hill, the inhabitants of M------, one mile from the lines of the Bois-le-Pretre, did a thriving business selling fruit to the soldiers, and I once saw an old peasant woman, who was digging potatoes in her garden when a small shell burst about two hundred feet from her, shake her fist toward the German lines, mutter something, and plod angrily home to her cellar. There are rarely any children close to the trenches, but in villages that are only occasionally shelled, the school is open, and the class hurries to the cellar at the first alarm.

The lieutenant of the American Section, a young Frenchman who spoke English not only fluently, but also with distinction, came to Nancy to take me to the front. It was a clear, sunny morning, and the rumble of the commercial life of Nancy, somewhat later in starting than our own, was just beginning to be heard. Across the street from the breakfast-room of the hotel, a young woman wearing a little black cape over her shoulders rolled up the corrugated iron shutter of a confectioner's shop and began to set the window with the popular patriotic candy boxes, aluminum models of a "seventy-five" shell tied round with a bow of narrow tricolor ribbon; a baker's boy in a white apron and blue jumpers went by carrying a basket of bread on his head; and from the nearby tobacconist's, a spruce young lieutenant dressed in a black uniform emerged lighting a cigarette. At nine in the morning I was contemplating a side street of busy, orderly, sunlit Nancy; that night I was in a cellar seeking refuge from fire shells.

"Please give me all your military papers," said my officer. I handed over all the cards, permits, and licenses that had been given me, and he examined them closely.

"Allons, let us go," he said to his chauffeur, a young soldier wearing the insignia of the motor-transportation corps.

"How long does it take us to get to the lines, mon lieutenant?"

"About an hour. Our headquarters are thirty kilometres distant."

The big, war-gray Panhard began to move. I looked round, eager to notice anything that marked our transition from peace to war. Beyond the Nancy, built in the Versailles style by the exiled Stanislaus, lay the industrial Nancy which has grown up since the development of the iron mines of French Lorraine in the eighties. Through this ugly huddle we passed first: there were working men on the sidewalks, gamins in the gutters,--nothing to remind one of the war.

"Halt!"

At a turn in the road near the outskirts of the city, a sentry, a small, gray-haired man, had stepped out before the car. From the door of a neighboring wineshop, a hideous old woman, her uncombed, tawny yellow hair messed round her coarse, shiny face, came out to look at us.

"Your papers, please," said a red-faced, middle-aged sergeant wearing a brown corduroy uniform, who, walking briskly on enormous fat legs, had followed the sentry out into the street. The lieutenant produced the military permit to travel in the army zone--the ordre de mouvement, a printed form on a blue sheet about the size of a leaf of typewriter paper.

"Pass," said the sergeant, and saluted. The sentry retired to his post on the sidewalk. At the door of the wineshop the woman continued to stare at us with an animal curiosity. Possibly our English-like uniforms had attracted her attention; the French are very curious about les Anglais. Over the roof of an ugly row of working men's barracks, built of mortar and trimmed with dingy brick, came the uproar of a great industry, the humming clang of saws, the ringing of iron on iron, and the heart-beat thump of a great hammer that shook the earth. In a vast, detached building five great furnaces were crowned with tufts of pinkish fire, workmen were crossing the cindery yard dragging little carts and long strips of iron, and a long line of open freight cars was being emptied of coal.

"They are making shells," said the lieutenant in the tone that he might have said, "They are making candy."

Another sentry held us up at the bridge where the road crosses the Moselle as it issues from the highlands to the southwest.

Beyond the bridge, running almost directly north to Metz, lay the historic valley of the Moselle. Great, bare hills, varying between seven hundred and a thousand feet in height, and often carved by erosion into strange, high triangles and abrupt mesas, formed the valley wall. The ground color of the hills was a warm buff-brown with a good deal of iron-red in it, and the sky above was of a light, friendly blue. A strange, Egyptian emerald of new wheat, a certain deep cobalt of cloud shadows, and a ruddy brownness of field and moor are the colors of Lorraine. Here and there, on the meadows of the river and the steep flanks of the hills, were ancient, red-roofed villages. Across the autumnal fields the smoke and flame of squalid Pompey loomed strangely.

There were signs of the war at Marbache, fourteen kilometres from Nancy, slight signs, to be sure, but good ones--the presence of a military smithy for the repair of army wagons, several of which stood by on rusty wheels, and a view of some twenty or thirty artillery caissons parked under the trees. But it was at B------, sixteen kilometres from Nancy, and sixteen from the lines, that I first felt the imminence of the war. The morning train from Nancy had just stopped, to go no farther for fear of shells, and beyond the station the tracks of the once busy Nancy-Metz railroad advanced, rusty, unused, and overgrown with grass, into the danger zone. Far behind now lay civilian Pompey, and Marbache shared by soldiers and civilians. B------was distinctly a village of the soldiery. The little hamlet, now the junction where the wagon-trains supplying the soldiery meet the great artery of the railroad, was built on the banks of a canal above the river. The color of these villages in Lorraine is rather lovely, for the walls of the houses, built of the local buff-yellow stone and ferrous sand, are of a warm, brown tone that goes well with the roofs of claret-red tile and the brown landscape. A glorious sky of silvery white cloud masses, pierced with sunlight and islanded with soft blue, shone over the soldier village. There were no combatants in it when we passed through, only the old poilus who drove the wagons to the trenches and the army hostlers who looked after the animals. There were pictures of soldier grooms leading horses down a narrow, slimy street between brown, mud-spattered walls to a drinking-trough; of horses lined up along a house wall being briskly curry-combed by big, thick-set fellows in blousy white overalls and blue fatigue caps; and of doors of stables opening on the road showing a bedding of brown straw on the earthen floor. There was a certain stench, too, the smell of horse-fouled mud that mixed with that odor I later was able to classify as the smell of war. For the war has a smell that clings to everything miltary, fills the troop-trains, hospitals, and cantonments, and saturates one's own clothing, a smell compounded of horse, chemicals, sweat, mud, dirt, and human beings. At the guarded exit of the village to the shell zone was a little military cemetery in which rows of wooden crosses stood with the regularity of pins in a paper.

Two kilometres farther on, at Dieulouard, we drew into the shell zone. A cottage had been struck the day before, and the shell, arriving by the roof, had blown part of the front wall out into the street. In the facade of the house, to the left of a door hanging crazily on its hinges, an irregular oval hole, large enough to drive a motor-car through, rose from the ground and came to a point just below the overhang of the roof. The edges of the broken stone were clean and new in contrast to the time-soiled outer wall of the dwelling.

A pile of this clean stone lay on the ground at the outer opening of the orifice, mixed with fragments of red tiles.

"They killed two there yesterday," said the lieutenant, pointing out the debris.

The village, a farming hamlet transformed by the vicinity of a great foundry into something neither a village nor a town, was full of soldiers; there were soldiers in the streets, soldiers standing in doorways, soldiers cooking over wood fires, soldiers everywhere. And looking at the muddy village-town full of men in uniforms of blue, old uniforms of blue, muddy uniforms of blue, in blue that was blue-gray and blue-green from wear and exposure to the weather, I realized that the old days of beautiful, half-barbaric uniforms were gone forever, and that, in place of the old romantic war of cavalry charges and great battles in the open, a new, more terrible war had been created, a war that had not the chivalric externals of the old.

After Dieulouard began the swathe of stillness.

Following the western bank of the canal of the Moselle the road made a great curve round the base of a hill descending to the river, and then mounted a little spur of the valley wall. Beyond the spur the road went through lonely fields, in which were deserted farmhouses surrounded by acres of neglected vines, now rank and Medusa-like in their weedy profusion. Every once in a while, along a rise, stood great burlap screens so arranged one behind the other as to give the effect of a continuous line when seen from a certain angle.

"What are those for?"

"To hide the road from the Germans. Do you see that little village down there on the crest? The Boches have an observatory there, and shell the road whenever they see anything worth shelling."

A strange stillness pervaded the air; not a stillness of death and decay, but the stillness of life that listens. The sun continued to shine on the brown moorland hills across the gray-green river, the world was quite the same, yet one sensed that something had changed. A village lay ahead of us, disfigured by random shells and half deserted. Beyond the still, shell-spattered houses, a great wood rose, about a mile and a half away, on a ridge that stood boldly against the sky. Running from the edge of the trees down across an open slope to the river was a brownish line that stood in a little contrast to the yellower grass. Suddenly, there slowly rose from this line a great puff of grayish-black smoke which melted away in the clear, autumnal air.

"See," said our lieutenant calmly, with no more emotion than he would have shown at a bonfire--"those are the German trenches. We have just fired a shell into them."

Two minutes more took us into the dead, deserted city of Pont-a-Mousson. The road was now everywhere screened carefully with lengths of light-brown burlap, and there was not a single house that did not bear witness to the power of a shell. The sense of "the front" began to possess me, never to go, the sense of being in the vicinity of a tremendous power. A ruined village, or a deserted town actually on the front does not bring to mind any impression of decay, for the intellect tends rather to consider t\& means by which the destruction has been accomplished. One sees villages of the swathes so completely blown to pieces that they are literally nothing but earthy mounds of rubbish, and seeing them thus, in a plain still fiercely disputed night and day between one's own side and the invisible enemy, the mind feels itself in the presence of force, titanic, secret, and hostile.

Beyond Pont-a-Mousson the road led directly to the trenches of the Bois-le-Pretre, less than half a mile away. But the disputed trenches were hidden behind the trees, and I could not see them. Through the silence of the deserted town sounded the muffled boom of shells and trench engines bursting in the wood beyond, and every now and then clouds of gray-black smoke from the explosion would rise above the brown leaves of the ash trees. The smoke of these explosions rose straight upwards in a foggy column, such as a locomotive might make if, halted on its tracks somewhere in the wood, it had put coal on its fires.

With the next day I began my service at the trenches, but the war began for me that very night.

A room in a bourgeois flat on the third floor of a deserted apartment house had been assigned me. It was nine o'clock, and I was getting ready to roll up in my blankets and go to sleep. Beneath the starlit heavens the street below was black as pitch save when a trench light, floating serenely down the sky, illuminated with its green-white glow the curving road and the line of dark, abandoned, half-ruinous villas. There was not a sound to be heard outside of an occasional rifle shot in the trenches, sounding for all the world like the click of giant croquet balls. I went round to the rear of the house and looked out of the kitchen windows to the lines. A little action, some quarrel of sentries, perhaps, was going on behind the trees, just where the wooded ridge sloped to the river. Trench light after trench light rose, showing the disused railroad track running across the un-harvested fields. Gleaming palely through the French window at which I was standing, the radiance revealed the deserted kitchen, the rusty stove, the dusty pans, and the tarnished water-tap above the stone sink. The hard, wooden crash of grenades broke upon my ears.

My own room was lit by the yellow flame of a solitary candle, rising, untroubled by the slightest breath of wind, straight into the air. A large rug of old-rose covered the floor, an old-rose velvet canopy draped a long table, hanging down at the corners in straight, heavy creases, and the wallpaper was a golden yellow with faint stripes of silvery-gray glaze. By the side of the wooden bed stood a high cabinet holding about fifty terra-cotta and porcelain figurines, shiny shepherdesses with shiny pink cheeks, Louis XV peasants with rakes on their shoulders, and three little dogs made of a material the color of cocoa. The gem of the collection was an eighteenth-century porcelain of a youth and a maid sitting on opposite sides of a curved bench over whose center rose a blossoming bush. The youth, dressed in black, and wearing yellow stockings, looked with an amorous smile at the girl in her gorgeous dress of flowering brocade.

A marbly-white fireplace stood in the corner, overhung by a great Louis XV mirror with a gilt frame of rich, voluptuous curves. On the mantel lay a scarf of old-rose velvet smelling decidedly musty. Alone, apart, upon this mantel, as an altar, stood a colored plaster bust of Jeanne d'Arc, showing her in the beauty of her winsome youth. The pale, girlish face dominated the shadowy room with its dreamy, innocent loveliness.

There came a knock at the door, and so still was the town and the house that the knock had the effect of something dramatic and portentous. A big man, with bulging, pink cheeks, a large, chestnut mustache, and brown eyes full of philosophic curiosity, stood in the doorway. The uniform that he was wearing was unusually neat and clean.

"So you are the American I am to have as neighbor," said he.

"Yes," I replied.

"I am the caporal in charge of the depot of the engineers in the cellar," continued my visitor, "and I thought I'd come in and see how you were."

I invited him to enter.

"Do you find yourself comfortable here, son?"

"Yes. I consider myself privileged to have the use of the room. Have a cigarette?"

"Are these American cigarettes?"

"Yes."

"Your American tobacco is fine, son. But in America everybody is a millionaire and has the best of everything--isn't that so? I should like to go to America."

"A Frenchman is never happy out of France."

Comfortably seated in a big, ugly chair, he puffed his cigarette and meditated.

"Perhaps you are right," he admitted. "We Frenchmen love the good things, and think we can get them in France better than anywhere else. The solid satisfactions of life--good wine--good cheese." He paused. "You see, son, all that (tout ca) is an affair of mine--in civilian life (dans le civil) I am a grocer at Macon in Bourgogne."

For a little while we talked of Burgundy, which I had often visited in my student days at Lyons. There came another pause, and the Burgundian said:--

"Well, what do you think of this big racket (ce grand fracas)?"

"I have not seen enough of it to say."

"Well, I think you are going to get a taste of it to-night. I heard our artillery men (nos artiflots) early this morning firing their long-range cannon, and every time they do that the Boches throw shells into Pont-a-Mousson. I have been expecting an answer all day. If they start in to-night, get up and come down cellar, son. This house was struck by a shell two weeks ago."

The shadowy, candlelit room and the dark city became at his words more mysterious and hostile. The atmosphere seemed pervaded by some obscure, endless, dreadful threat. It was getting toward ten o'clock.

"Is this the only room you have? I have never been in this suite."

"No, there is another room. Would you like to see it?"

He followed me into a small chamber from which everything had been stripped except a bedside table, a chair, and a crayon portrait of a woman. The picture, slightly tinted with flesh color, was that of a bourgeoise on the threshold of the fifties, and the still candle-flame brought out in distinct relief the heavy, obese countenance, the hair curled in artificial ringlets, and the gold crucifix which she wore on her large bosom. The Burgundian's attention centered on this picture, which he examined with the air of a connoisseur of female beauty.

"Lord, how ugly she is!" he exclaimed. "She might well have stayed. Such an old dragon would have no reason to fear the Boches." And he laughed heartily from his rich lips and pulled his mustache.

"Don't forget to hurry to the cellar, son," he called as he went away.

At his departure the lonely night closed in on me again. Far, far away sounded the booming of cannon.

I am a light sleeper, and the arrival of the first shell awakened me. Kicking off my blankets, I sat up in bed just in time to catch the swift ebb of a heavy concussion. A piece of glass, dislodged from a broken pane by the tremor, fell in a treble tinkle to the floor. For a minute or two there was a full, heavy silence, and then several objects rolled down the roof and fell over the gutters into the street. It sounded as if some one had emptied a hodful of coal onto the house-roof from the height of the clouds. Another silence followed. Suddenly it was broken by a swift, complete sound, a heavy boom-roar, and on the heels of this noise came a throbbing, whistling sigh that, at first faint as the sound of ocean on a distant beach, increased with incredible speed to a whistling swish, ending in a HISH of tremendous volume and a roaring, grinding burst. The sound of a great shell is never a pure bang; one hears, rather, the end of the arriving HISH, the explosion, and the tearing disintegration of the thick wall of iron in one grinding hammer-blow of terrific violence. On the heels of this second shell came voices in the dark street, and the rosy glow of fire from somewhere behind. More lumps, fragments of shell that had been shot into the air by the explosion, rained down upon the roof. I got up and went to the kitchen window. A house on one of the silent streets between the city and the lines was on fire, great volumes of smoke were rolling off into the starlit night, and voices were heard all about murmuring in the shadows. I hurried on my clothes and went down to the cellar.

The light of two candles hanging from a shelf in loops of wire revealed a clean, high cellar; a mess of straw was strewn along one wall, and a stack of shovels and picks, some of them wrapped in paper, was banked against the other. In the straw lay three oldish men, fully clad in the dark-blue uniform which in old times had signaled the Engineer Corps; one dozed with his head on his arm, the other two were stretched out flat in the mysterious grossness of sleep. A door from the cellar to a sunken garden was open, and through this opening streamed the intense radiance of the rising fire. At the opening stood three men, my visitor of the evening, a little, wrinkled man with Napoleon III whiskers and imperial, and an old, dwarfish fellow with a short neck, a bullet head, and close-clipped hair. Catching sight of me, the Burgundian said:--

"Well, son, you see it is hammering away (ca tape) ce soir."

Hearing another shell, he slammed the door, and stepped to the right behind the stone wall of the cellar.

"Very bad," croaked the dwarf. "The Boches are throwing fire shells."

"And they will fire shrapnel at the poor bougres who have to put out the fires," said the little man with the imperial.

"So they will, those knaves," croaked the dwarf in a voice entirely free from any emotion. "That fire must be down on the Boulevard Ney," said the bearded man.

"There is another beginning just to the right," said the Burgundian in the tone of one retailing interesting but hardly useful information.

"There will be others," croaked the dwarf, who, leaning against the cellar wall, was trying to roll a cigarette with big, square, fumbling fingers. And looking at a big, gray-haired man in the hay, who had turned over and was beginning to snore, he added: "Look at the new man. He sleeps well, that fellow" (ce type la).

"He looks like a Breton," said the man with the imperial.

"An Auvergnat--an Auvergnat," replied the dwarf in a tone that was meant to be final.

The soldier, who had just been sent down from Paris to take the place of another recently invalided home, snored on, unconscious of our scrutiny. The light from the fires outside cast a rosy glow on his weather-worn features and sparse, silvery hair. His own curiosity stirred, the corporal looked at his list.

"He came from Lyons," he announced. "His name is Alphonse Reboulet."

"I am glad he is not an Auvergnat," growled the dwarf. "We should have all had fleas."

A shell burst very near, and a bitter odor of explosives came swirling through the doorway. A fragment of the shell casing struck a window above us, and a large piece of glass fell by the doorway and broke into splinters. The first fire was dying down, but two others were burning briskly. The soldiers waited for the end of the bombardment, as they might have waited for the end of a thunderstorm.

"Tiens--here comes the shrapnel," exclaimed the Burgundian. And he slammed the door swiftly.

A high, clear whistle cleaved the flame-lit sky, and about thirty small shrapnel shells burst beyond us.

"They try to prevent any one putting out the fires," said the Burgundian confidentially. "They get the range from the light of the flames."

Another dreadful rafale (volley) of shrapnel, at the rate of ten or fifteen a minute, came speeding from the German lines.

"They are firing on the other house, now."

"Who puts out the fires?"

"The territorials who police and clean up the town. Some of them live two doors below."

The Burgundian pointed down the garden to a door opening, like our own, on to an area below the level of the street. Suddenly, a gate opening on a back lane swung back, and two soldiers entered, one carrying the feet and the other the shoulders of a third. The body hung clumsily between them like a piece of old sacking.

"Tiens--someone is wounded," said the Burgundian. "Go, thou, Badel, and see who it is."

The dwarf plodded off obediently.

"It is Palester," he announced on his return, "the type that had the swollen jaw last month."

"What's the matter with him?"
"He's been killed."

Chapter IV
La Foret De Bois-Le-Pretre

Beginning at the right bank of the Meuse, a vast plateau of bare, desolate moorland sweeps eastward to the Moselle, and descends to the river in a number of great, wooded ridges perpendicular to the northward-flowing stream. The town of Pont-a-Mousson lies an apron of meadowland spread between two of these ridges, the ridge of Puvenelle and the ridge of the Bois-le-Pretre. The latter is the highest of all the spurs of the valley. Rising from the river about half a mile to the north of the city, it ascends swiftly to the level of the plateau, and was seen from our headquarters as a long, wooded ridge blocking the sky-line to the northwest. The hamlet of Maidieres, in which our headquarters were located, lies just at the foot of Puvenelle, at a point where the amphitheater of Pont-a-Mousson, crowding between the two ridges, becomes a steep-walled valley sharply tilted to the west.

The Bois-le-Pretre dominated at once the landscape and our minds. Its existence was the one great fact in the lives of some fifty thousand Frenchmen, Germans, and a handful of exiled Americans; it had dominated and ended the lives of the dead; it would dominate the imagination of the future. Yet, looking across the brown walls and claret roofs of the hamlet of Maidieres, there was nothing to be seen but a grassy slope, open fields, a reddish ribbon of road, a wreck of a villa burned by a fire shell, and a wood. The autumn had turned the leaves of the trees, seemingly without exception, to a leathery brown, and in almost all lights the trunks of the trees were a cold, purplish slate. Such was the forest which, battle-areas excepted, has cost more lives than any other point along the line. The wood had been contested trench by trench, literally foot by foot. It was at once the key to the Saint-Mihiel salient and the city of Metz.

The Saint-Mihiel salient--"the hernia," as the French call it--begins at the Bois-le-Pretre. Pivoting on The Wood, the lines turn sharply inland, cross the desolate plateau of La Woevre, attain the Meuse at Saint-Mihiel, turn again, and ascend the river to the Verdunois. The salient, as dangerous for the Germans as it is trouble-some for the French, represents the limit of a German offensive directed against Toul in October, 1914. That the French retreated was due to the fact that the pla-teau was insufficiently protected, many of the regiments having been rushed north to the great battle then raging on the Aisne.

Only one railroad center lies in the territory of the salient, Thiaucourt in Wo-evre. This pleasant little moorland town, locally famous for its wine, is connected with Metz by two single-track railroad lines, one coming via Conflans, and the other by Arnaville on the Moselle. At Vilcey-sur-Mad, these lines unite, and follow to Thiaucourt the only practicable railroad route, the valley of the Rupt (brook) de Mad.

Thus the domination of Thiaucourt, or the valley of the Rupt de Mad, by French artillery would break the railroad communications between the troops keeping the salient and their base of supplies, Metz. And the fate of Metz itself hangs on the control of the Bois-le-Pretre.

Metz is the heart of the German organization on the western front: the railroad center, the supply station, the troop depot. A blow at Metz would affect the security of every German soldier between Alsace and the Belgian frontier. But if the French can drive the Germans out of the Bois-le-Pretre and establish big howitzers on the crest the Germans are still holding, there will soon be no more Metz. The French guns will destroy the city as the German cannon destroyed Verdun.

When the Germans, therefore, retired to the trenches after the battles of Sep-tember and October, 1914, they took to the ground on the heights of the Bois-le-Pretre, a terrain far enough ahead of Thiaucourt and Metz to preserve these centers from the danger of being shelled. On the crest of the highest ridge along the valley, admirably ambushed in a thick forest, they waited for the coming of the French. And the French came.

They came, young and old, slum-dweller and country schoolmaster, rich young noble and Corsican peasant, to the storming of the wood, upheld by one vision, the unbroken, grassy slope that stretched from behind the German lines to the town of Thiaucourt. In the trenches behind the slaty trunks of the great ash trees, Bavar-ian peasants, Saxons, and round-headed Wurttem-burgers, the olive-green, jack-booted Boches, awaited their coming, determined to hold the wood, the salient, and the city.

A year later the Bois-le-Pretre (the Priest Wood), with its perfume of ecclesi-astical names that reminds one of the odor of incense in an old church, had become the Bois de la Mort (the Wood of Death).

The house in which our bureau was located was once the summer residence of a rich ironmaster who had fled to Paris at the beginning of the war. If there is an ar-chitectural style of German origin known as the "Neo-Classic," which affects large, windowless spaces framed in pilasters of tile, and decorations and insets of omelet-yellow and bottle-green glazed brick, "Wisteria Villa" is of that school. It stood be-hind a high wall of iron spikes on the road leading from Maidieres to the trenches, a high, Germano-Pompeian country house, topped by a roof rich in angles, absurd windows, and unexpected gables. There are huge, square, French-roofed houses in New England villages built by local richessimes of Grant's time, and still called by neighbors "the Jinks place" or the "Levi Oates place"; Wisteria Villa had something of the same social relation to the commune of Maidieres. Grotesque and ugly, it was not to be despised; it had character in its way.

Our social center was the dining-room of the villa. Exclusive of the kitchen range, it boasted the only stove in the house, a queerly shaped "Salamandre," a kind of Franklin stove with mica doors. The walls were papered an ugly chocolate brown with a good deal of red in it, and the borders, doors, and fireplace frame were stained a color trembling between mission green and oak brown. The room was rectangular and too high for its width. There were pictures. On each side of the fireplace, profiles toward the chimney, hung concave plaques of Dutch girls. To the left of the door was a yellowed etching of the tower of the chateau of Heidelberg, and to the right a very small oil painting, in an ornate gilt frame three inches deep, of a beach by moonlight. About two or three hundred books, bound in boards and red leather, stood behind the cracked glass of a bookcase in the corner; they were very "jeune fille," and only the romances of Georges Ohnet appeared to have been read. The thousand cupboards of the house were full of dusty knickknacks, old umbrellas, hats, account-books, and huge boxes holding the debris of sets of check-ers, dominoes, and ivory chessmen. An enlarged photograph of the family hung on the walls of a bedroom; it had been taken at somebody's marriage, and showed the group standing on the front steps, the same steps that were later to be blown to pieces by a shell. One saw the bride, the groom, and about twenty relatives, including a boy in short trousers, a wide, white collar, and an old-fashioned, fluffy bow tie. Anxious to be included in the picture, the driver of the bridal barouche has craned his neck forward. On the evidence of the costumes, the picture had been taken about 1902.

Our bureau in the cellar of Wisteria Villa was connected directly with the trenches. When a man had been wounded, he was carried to the poste de secours in the rear lines, and it was our duty to go to this trench post and carry the patient to the hospital at the nearest rail-head. The bureau of the Section was in charge of two Frenchmen who shared the labor of attending to the telephone and keeping the books.

A hundred yards beyond Wisteria Villa, at a certain corner, the principal road to the trenches divided into three branches, and in order to interfere as much as possible with communications, the Germans daily shelled this strategic point. A comrade and I had the curiosity to keep an exact record of a week's shelling. It must be remembered that the corner was screened from the Germans, who fired casually in the hope of hitting something and annoying the French. The cannons shelling the corner were usually "seventy-sevens," the German quick-firing pieces that correspond to the French "seventy-fives."

Monday, ten shells at 6.30, two at 7.10, five at 11.28, twenty at intervals between 2.15 and 2.45, a swift rafale of some sixteen at 4.12, another rafale of twenty at 8, and occasional shells between 9 and midnight.

Tuesday, two big shells at mid-day.

Wednesday, rafales at 9.14, 11, 2.18, 4.30, and 6.20.

Thursday--no shells.

Friday, twelve at intervals between 10.16 and 12.20. Solitary big shell at 1.05. Another big shell at 3. Some fifteen stray shells between 5 and midnight.

Saturday--no shells.

Sunday--About five shells an hour between 4 in the afternoon and midnight.

I give the number of shells falling at this corner as a concrete instance of what was happening at a dozen other points along the road. The fire of the German batteries was as capricious as the play of a search-light; one week, the corner and three or four other points would catch it, the next week the corner and another set of localities. And there were periods, sometimes ten days to two weeks long, when hardly a shell was fired at any road. Then, after a certain sense of security had begun to take form, a rafale would come screaming over, blow a horse and wagon to pieces, and leave one or two blue figures huddled in the mud. But the French replied to each shell and every rafale, in addition to firing at random all the day and a good deal of the night. There was hardly a night that Wisteria Villa did not rock to the sound of French guns fired at 2 and 3 in the morning. But the average day at Pont-a-Mousson was a day of random silences. The war had all the capriciousness of the sea--of uncertain weather. There were hours of calm in the day, during which the desolate silence of the front flooded swiftly over the landscape; there were interruptions of great violence, sometimes desultory, sometimes beginning, in obedience to a human will, at a certain hour. The outbreak would commence with the orderliness of a clock striking, and continue the greater part of the day, rocking the deserted town with its clamor. Hearing it, the soldiers en repos would say, talking of The Wood, "It sings (ca chante)," or, "It knocks (ca tape) up there to-day." The smoke of the bursting shells hung over The Wood in a darkish, gray-blue fog. But since The Wood had a personality for us, many would say simply, "Listen to The Wood."

The shell expresses one idea--energy. The cylinder of iron, piercing the air at a terrific speed, sings a song of swift, appalling energy, of which the final explosion is the only fitting culmination. One gets, too, an idea of an unbending volition in the thing. After a certain time at the front the ear learns to distinguish the sound of a big shell from a small shell, and to know roughly whether or not one is in the danger zone. It was a grim jest with us that it took ten days to qualify as a shell expert, and at the end of two weeks all those who qualified attended the funeral of those who had failed. Life at The Wood had an interesting uncertainty.

A quarter of a mile beyond the corner, on the slope of Puvenelle opposite The Wood, stood Montauville, the last habitable village of the region. To the south of it rose the wooded slopes of Puvenelle; to the north, seen across a marshy meadow, were the slope and the ridge of the Bois-le-Pretre. The dirty, mud-spattered village was caught between the leathery sweeps of two wooded ridges. Three winding roads, tramped into a pie of mire, crossed the grassy slope of The Wood, and disappeared into the trees at the top. Though less than a mile from the first German line, the village, because of its protection from shells by a spur of the Bois-le-Pretre, was in remarkably good condition; the only building to show conspicuous damage being the church, whose steeple had been twice struck. It was curious to see pigeons flying in and out of the belfry through the shell rents in the roof. Here and there, among the uncultivated fields of those who had fled, were the green fields of some one who had stayed. A woman of seventy still kept open her grocery shop; it was extraordinarily dirty, full of buzzing flies, and smelled of spilled wine.

"Why did you stay?" I asked her.

"Because I did not want to leave the village. Of course my daughter wanted me to come to Dijon. Imagine me in Dijon, I, who have been to Nancy only once! A fine figure I should make in Dijon in my sabots!"

"And you are not afraid of the shells?"

"Oh, I should be afraid of them if I ever went out in the street. But I never leave my shop."

And so she stayed, selling the three staples of the French front, Camembert cheese, Norwegian sardines, and cakes of chocolate. But Montauville was far from safe. It was there that I first saw a man killed. I had been talking to a sentry, a small young fellow of twenty-one or two, with yellow hair and gray-blue eyes full of weariness. He complained of a touch of jaundice, and wished heartily that the whole affaire--meaning the war in general--was finished. He was very anxious to know if the Americans thought the Boches were going to win. Some vague idea of winning the war just to get even with the Boches seemed to be in his mind. I assured him that American opinion was optimistic in regard to the chances of the Allies, and strolled away. Hardly had I gone ten feet, when a "seventy-seven" shell, arriving without warning, went Zip-bang, and, turning to crouch to the wall, I saw the sentry crumple up in the mud. It was as if he were a rubber effigy of a man blown up with air, and some one had suddenly ripped the envelope. His rifle fell from him, and he, bending from the waist, leaned face down into the mud. I was the first to get to him. The young, discontented face was full of the gray street mud, there was mud in the hollows of the eyes, in the mouth, in the fluffy mustache. A chunk of the shell had ripped open the left breast to the heart. Down his sleeve, as down a pipe, flowed a hasty drop, drop, drop of blood that mixed with the mire.

Several times a day, at stated hours, the numbers of German missiles that had fallen into the trenches of the Bois-le-Pretre, together with French answers to them, would be telephoned to headquarters. The soldier in charge of the telephone was an instructor in Latin in a French provincial university, a tall, stoop- shouldered man, with an indefinite, benevolent smile curiously framed on thin lips. Probably very much of a scholar by training and feeling, he had accepted his military destiny, and was as much a poilu as anybody. During his leisure hours he was busy writing a "Comparison of the Campaign on the Marne and the Aisne with Caesar's battles against the Belgian Confederacy." He had a paper edition of the Gallic Wars which he carried round with him. One day he explained his thesis to me. He drew a plan with a green pencil on a piece of paper.

"See, mon ami," he exclaimed, "here is the Aisne, Caesar's Axona; here is Berry-au-Bac; here was Caesar, here were the invaders, here was General French, here Foch, here Von Kluck. Curious, isn't it--two thousand years afterward?" His eyes for an instant filled with dreamy perplexity. A little while later I would hear him mechanically telephoning. "Poste A--five 'seventy-seven' shells, six mines, twelve trench shells; answer--ten 'seventy-five' shells, eight mines, eighteen trench shells; Poste B--two 'seventy-seven' shells, one mine, six grenades; answer--fifteen 'seventy-five' shells; Poste C--one 'two hundred and ten' shell, fifty mines; answer--sixty mines; Poste D--"

At Dieulouard I had entered the shell zone; at Pont-a-Mousson, I crossed the borders of the zone of quiet; at Montauville began the last zone--the zone of invisibility and violence. Civilian life ended at the western end of the village street with the abruptness of a man brought face to face with a high wall. Beyond the village a road was seen climbing the grassy slope of Puvenelle, to disappear as it neared the summit of the ridge in a brown wood. It was just an ordinary hill road of Lorraine, but the fact that it was the direct road to the trenches invested this climbing, winding, silent length with extraordinary character. The gate of the zone of violence, every foot of it bore some scar of the war, now trivial, now gigantic--always awesome in the power and volition it revealed. One passed from the sight of a brown puddle, scooped in the surface of the street by an exploding shell, to a view of a magnificent ash tree splintered by some projectile. It is a very rare thing to see a sinister landscape, but this whole road was sinister. I used to discuss this sinister quality with a distinguished French artist who as a poilu was the infirmier, or medical service man, attached to a squad of engineers working in a quarry frequently shelled. In this frightful place we discussed la qualite du sinistre dans l'art (the sinister in art) as calmly as if we were two Parisian critics sitting on the benches of the Luxembourg Gardens. As the road advanced into the wood, there was hardly a wayside tree that had not been struck by a shell. Branches hung dead from trees, twigs had been lopped off by stray fragments, great trunks were split apart as if by lightning. "Nature as Nature is never sinister," said the artist; "it is when there is a disturbance of the relations between Nature and human life that you have the sinister. Have you ever seen the villages beyond Ravenna overwhelmed by the bogs? There you see the sinister. Here Man is making Nature unlivable for Man." He stroked his fine silky beard meditatively--"This will all end when the peasants plant again." As we talked, a shell, intended for the batteries behind, burst high above us.

Skirting the ravine, now wooded, between Puvenelle and the Bois-le-Pretre, the road continued westward till it emerged upon the high plateau of La Woevre; the last kilometre being in full view of the Germans entrenched on the ridge across the rapidly narrowing, rising ravine. Along this visible space the trees and bushes by the roadside were matted by shell fire into an inextricable confusion of destruction, and through the wisps and splinters of this ruin was seen the ridge of the Bois-le-Pretre rapidly attaining the level of the moor. At length the forest of Puvenelle, the ravine, and the Bois-le-Pretre ended together in a rolling sweep of furzy fields cut off to the west and north by a vast billow of the moor which, like the rim of a saucer, closed the wide horizon. Continuing straight ahead, the Puvenelle road mounted this rise, dipped and disappeared. Halfway between the edge of the forest of Puvenelle and this crest stood an abandoned inn, a commonplace building made of buff-brown moorland stone trimmed with red brick. Close by this inn, at right angles to the Puvenelle road, another road turned to the north and likewise disappeared over the lift in the moor. At the corner stood a government signpost of iron slightly bent back, bearing in gray-white letters on its clay-blue plaque the legend--Thiaucourt, 12 kilometres Metz, 25 kilometres.

There was not a soul anywhere in sight; I was surrounded with evidences of terrific violence--the shattered trees, the shell holes in the road, the brown-lipped craters in the earth of the fields, the battered inn; but there was not a sign of the creators of this devastation. A northwest wind blew in great salvos across the mournful, lonely plateau, rippling the furze, and brought to my ears the pounding of shells from behind the rise. When I got to this rim a soldier, a big, blond fellow of the true Gaulois type with drooping yellow mustaches, climbed slowly out of a hole in the ground. The effect was startling. I had arrived at the line where the earth of France completely swallows up the army. This disappearance of life in a decor of intense action is one of the most striking things of the war. All about in the surface of the earth were little, square, sooty holes that served as chimneys, and here and there rectangular, grave-like openings in the soil showing three or four big steps descending to a subterranean hut. Fifty feet away not a sign of human life could be distinguished. Six feet under the ground, framed in the doorway of a hut, a young, black-haired fellow in a dark-brown jersey stood smiling pleasantly up at us; it was he who was to be my guide to the various postes and trenches that I had need to know. He came up to greet me.

"Better bring him down here," growled a voice from somewhere in the earth. "There have been bullets crossing the road all afternoon."

"I am going to show him the Quart-en-Reserve first."

The Quart-en-Reserve (Reserved Quarter) was the section of the Bois-le-Pretre which, because of its situation on the crest of the great ridge, had been the most fiercely contested. We crept up on the edge of the ridge and looked over. An open, level field some three hundred yards wide swept from the Thiaucourt road to the edges of the Bois-le-Pretre; across this field ran in the most confused manner a strange pattern of brown lines that disappeared among the stumps and poles of the haggard wood to the east. To the northwest of this plateau, on the road ahead of us, stood a ruined village caught in the torment of the lines. Here and there, in some twenty or thirty places scattered over the scarred plateau, the smoke of trench shells rose in little curling puffs of gray-black that quickly dissolved in the wind.

"The Quart is never quiet," said my guide. "It is now half ours, half theirs."

Close to the ground, a blot of light flashed swifter than a stroke of lightning, and a heavier, thicker smoke rolled away.

"That is one of ours. We are answering their trench shells with an occasional 'one hundred and twenty."

"How on earth is it that everybody is not killed?"

"Because the regiment has occupied the Quart so long that we know every foot, every turn, every shelter of it. When we see a trench shell coming, we know just where to go. It is only the newcomers who get killed. Two months past, when a new regiment occupied the Quart during our absence en repos, it lost twenty-five men in one day."

The first trench that I entered was a simple trench about seven feet deep, with no trimmings whatsoever, just such a trench as might have been dug for the accommodation of a large water conduit. We walked on a narrow board walk very slippery with cheesy, red-brown mire. From time to time the hammer crash of a shell sounded uncomfortably near, and bits of dirt and pebbles, dislodged by the concussion, fell from the wall of the passage. The only vista was the curving wall of the long communication trench and the soft sky of Lorraine, lit with the pleasant sunlight of middle afternoon, and islanded with great golden-white cloud masses. My guide and I might have been the last persons left in a world of strange and terrible noises. The boyau (communication trench) began to turn and wind about in the most perplexing manner, and we entered a veritable labyrinth. This extraordinary, baffling complexity is due primarily to the fact that the trenches advance and retreat, rise and fall, in order to take advantage of the opportunities for defense afforded by every change in the topography of the region. I remember one area along the front consisting of two round, grassy hills divided by a small, grassy valley whose floor rose gently to a low ridge connecting the two heights. In this terrain the defensive line began on the first hill as a semicircle edging the grassy slopes presented to the enemy, then retreated, sinking some forty feet, to take advantage of the connecting link of upland at the head of the ravine, and took semicircular form again on the flat, broad summit of the second hill. In the meadows at the base of these hills a brook flowing from the ravine had created a great swamp, somewhat in the shape of a wedge pointing outward from the mouth of the valley. The lines of the enemy, edging this tract of mire, were consequently in the shape of an open V. Thus the military situation at this particular point may be pictorially represented by a salient semicircle, a dash, and another salient semicircle faced by a wide, open V. Imagine such a situation complicated by offensive and counter-offensive, during which the French have seized part of the hills and the German part of the plain, till the whole region is a madman's maze of barbed wire, earthy lines, trenches,-- some of them untenable by either side and still full of the dead who fell in the last combat,--shell holes, and fortified craters. Such was something of the situation in that wind-swept plain at the edge of the Bois-le-Pretre. I leave for other chapters the account of an average day in the trenches and the story of the great German attack, preferring to tell here of the general impressions made by the appearance of the trenches themselves. Two pictures stand out, particularly, the dead on the barbed wire, and the village called "Fey au Rats" at night.

"The next line is the first line. Speak in whispers now, for if the Boches hear us we shall get a shower of hand-grenades."

I turned into a deep, wide trench whose floor had been trodden into a slop of cheesy, brown mire which clung to the big hobnailed boots of the soldiers. Every foot or so along the parapet there was a rifle slit, made by the insertion of a wedge-shaped wooden box into the wall of brownish sandbags, and the sentries stood about six feet apart. The trench had the hushed quiet of a sickroom.

"Do you want to see the Boches? Here; come, put your eye to this rifle slit."

A horizontal tangle of barbed wire lay before me, the shapeless gully of an empty trench, and, thirty-five feet away, another blue-gray tangle of barbed wire and a low ripple of the brownish earth. As I looked, one of the random silences of the front stole swiftly into the air. French trench and German trench were perfectly silent; you could have heard the ticking of a watch.

"You never see them?"

"Only when we attack them or they attack us."

An old poilu, with a friendly smile revealing a jagged reef of yellow teeth, whispered to me amiably:--

"See them? Good Lord, it's bad enough to smell them. You ought to thank the good God, young man, that the wind is carrying it over our heads."

"Any wounded to-day?"

"Yes; a corporal had his leg ripped up about half an hour ago."

At a point a mile or so farther down the moor I looked again out of a rifle box. No Man's Land had widened to some three hundred feet of waving furze, over whose surface gusts of wind passed as over the surface of the sea. About fifty feet from the German trenches was a swathe of barbed wire supported on a row of five stout, wooden posts. So thickly was the wire strung that the eye failed to distinguish the individual filaments and saw only the rows of brown-black posts filled with a steely purple mist. Upon this mist hung masses of weather-beaten blue rags whose edges waved in the wind.

"Des camarades" (comrades), said my guide very quietly.

A month later I saw the ruined village of Fey-en-Haye by the light of the full golden shield of the Hunters' Moon. The village had been taken from the Germans in the spring, and was now in the French lines, which crossed the village street and continued right on through the houses. "The first village on the road to Metz" had tumbled, in piles and mounds of rubbish, out on a street grown high with grass. Moonlight poured into the roofless cottages, escaping by shattered walls and jagged rents, and the mounds of debris took on fantastic outlines and cast strange shadows. In the middle of the village street stood two wooden crosses marking the graves of soldiers. It was the Biblical "Abomination of Desolation."

Looking at Fey from the end of the village street, I slowly realized that it was not without inhabitants. Wandering through the grass, scurrying over the rubbish heaps, running in and out of the crumbling thresholds were thousands and thousands of rats.

Across the bright sky came a whirring hum, the sound of the motors of aeroplanes on the way to bombard the railroad station at Metz. I looked up, but there was nothing to be seen. The humming died away. The bent signpost at the corner of the deserted moorland road, with its arrow and its directions, somehow seemed a strange, shadowy symbol of the impossibility of the attainment of many human aspirations.

Chapter V
The Trenches In The "Wood Of Death"

So great has been the interest in the purely military side of the struggle that one is apt to forget that the war is worth study as the supreme occupation of many great nations, whose every energy, physical, moral, and economic, has been put to its service, and relentlessly tested in its fiery furnace. A future historian may find the war more interesting, when considered as the supreme achievement of the industrial civilization of the nineteenth and twentieth centuries, than as a mere vortex in the age-old ocean of European political strife. There is something awe-inspiring in the spectacle of all the continuous and multitudinous activity of a great nation feeding, by a thousand channels, a thousand rills, to the embattled furrows of the zone of violence.

By a strange decree of fate, a new warfare has come into being, admirably adapted to the use and the testing of all our faculties, organizations, and inventions--trench warfare. The principal element of this modern warfare is lack of mobility.

The lines advance, the lines retreat, but never once, since the establishment of the present trench swathe, have the lines of either combatant been pushed clear out of the normal zone of hostilities. The fierce, invisible combats are limited to the first-line positions, averaging a mile each way behind No Man's Land. This stationary character has made the war a daily battle; it has robbed war of all its ancient panoply, its cavalry, its uniforms brilliant as the sun, and has turned it into the national business. I dislike to use the word "business," with its usual atmosphere of orderly bargaining; I intend rather to call up an idea more familiar to American minds--the idea of a great intricate organization with a corporate volition. The war of to-day is a business, the people are the stockholders, and the object of the organization is the wisest application of violence to the enemy.

To this end, in numberless secteurs along the front, special narrow-gauge railroad lines have been built directly from the railroad station at the edge of the shell zone to the artillery positions. To this end the trenches have been gathered into a special telephone system so that General Joffre at Chantilly can talk to any officers or soldiers anywhere along the great swathe. The food, supplies, clothing, and ammunition are delivered every day at the gate of the swathe, and calmly redistributed to the trenches by a sort of military express system.

Only one thing ever disturbs the vast, orderly system. The bony fingers of Death will persist in getting into the cogs of the machine.

The front is divided, according to military exigencies, into a number of roughly equal lengths called secteurs. Each secteur is an administrative unit with its own government and its own system adapted to the local situation. The heart of this unit is the railroad station at which the supplies arrive for the shell zone; in a normal secteur, one military train arrives every day bringing the needed supplies, and one hospital train departs, carrying the sick and wounded to the hospitals. The station at the front is always a scene of considerable activity, especially when the train arrives; there are pictures of old poilus in red trousers pitching out yellow hay for the horses, commissary officers getting their rations, and artilleurs stacking shells.

The train not being able to continue into the shell zone, the supplies are carried to the distributing station at the trenches in a convoy of wagons, called the ravitaillement. Every single night, somewhere along the road, each side tries to smash up the other's ravitaillement. To avoid this, the ravitaillement wagons start at different hours after dark, now at dusk, now at midnight. Sometimes, close by the trenches on a clear, still night, the plashing and creaking of the enemy's wagons can be heard through the massacred trees. I remember being shelled along one bleak stretch of moorland road just after a drenching December rain. The trench lights rising over The Wood, three miles away, made the wet road glow with a tarnished glimmer, and burnished the muddy pools into mirrors of pale light. The ravitaillement creaked along in the darkness. Suddenly a shell fell about a hundred yards away, and the wagons brought up jerkily, the harnesses rattling. For ten minutes the Germans shelled the length of road just ahead of us, but no shell came closer to us than the first one. About thirty "seventy-seven" shells burst, some on the road, some on the edges of the fields; we saw them as flashes of reddish-violet light close to the ground. In the middle of the melee a trench light rose, showing the line of halted gray wagons, the motionless horses, and the helmeted drivers. The whole affair passed in silence. When it was judged that the last shell had fallen, whips cracked like pistol shots, and the line lumbered on again.

The food came to us fresh every day in a freight car fitted up like a butcher's shop, in charge of a poilu who was a butcher in civilian life. "So many men--so many grammes," and he would cut you off a slice. There was a daily potato ration, and a daily extra, this last from a list ten articles long which began again every ten days, and included beans, macaroni, lentils, rice, and cheese. The French army is very well and plenteously fed. Coffee, sugar, wine, and even tea are ungrudgingly furnished. These foods are taken directly to the rear of the trenches where the regimental cooks have their traveling kitchens. Once the food is prepared, the cooks--the beloved cuistots--take it to the trenches in great, steaming kettles and distribute it to the men individually. As for clothing, every regiment has a regimental tailor shop and supply of uniforms in the village where they go to repos. I have often seen the soldier tailor of one of the regiments, a little Alsatian Jew, sewing up the shell rents in a comrade's greatcoat. He had his shop in a pleasant kitchen, and used to sit beside the fire sewing as calmly as an old woman.

The sanitary arrangements of the trenches are the usual army latrines, and very severe punishments are inflicted for any fouling.

If a man is wounded, the medical service man of his squad (infirmier), or one of the stretcher-bearers (brancardiers), takes him as quickly as possible to the regimental medical post in the rear lines. If the trench is getting heavily shelled, and the wound is slight, the attendant takes the man to a shelter and applies first aid until a time comes when he and his patient can proceed to the rear with reasonable safety. At this rear post the regimental surgeon cleans the wound, stops the bleeding, and sends for the ambulance, which, at the Bois-le-Pretre, came right into the heart of the trenches by sunken roads that were in reality broad trenches. The man is then taken to the hospital that his condition requires, the slightly wounded to one hospital, and those requiring an operation to another. The French surgical hospitals all along the front are marvels of cleanliness and order. The heart of each hospital is the power plant, which sterilizes the water, runs the electric lights, and works the X-ray generator. Mounted on an automobile body, it is always ready to decamp in case the locality gets too dangerous. You find these great, lumbering affairs, half steamroller, half donkey-engine, in the courtyards of old castles, schools, and great private houses close by the front.

The first-line trenches, in a position at all contested, are very apt still to preserve the hurried arrangement of their first plan, which is sometimes hardly any plan at all. It must be admitted that the Germans have the advantage in the great majority of places, for theirs was the first choice, and they entrenched themselves, as far as possible, along the crests of the eastern hills of France, in a line long prepared for just such an exigency. It has been the frightfully difficult task of the Allies, these two years, not only to hold the positions at the foot of these hills, in which they were at a tactical disadvantage, all their movements being visible to the Boches on the crests above them, but also to attack an enemy entrenched in a strong position of his own choosing. To-day at one point along the line, the French and Germans may share the dominating crest of a position, at another point, they may be equally matched, and at another, such as Les Eparges, the French, after fearful losses, have carried the coveted eminence. One phase of the business of violence is the work of the military undertaker attached to each secteur, who writes down in his little red book the names of the day's dead, and arranges for the wooden cross at the head of each fresh grave. Every day along the front is a battle in which thousands of men die.

The eastern hills of France, those pleasant rolling heights above Rheims, Verdun, and old, provincial Pont-a-Mousson, have been literally gorged with blood. It being out of the question to strengthen or rectify very much the front-line trenches close to the enemy, the effort has taken place in the rear lines. Wherever there is a certain security, the rear lines of all the important strategic points have been converted into veritable subterranean fortresses. The floor plan of these trenches is an adaptation of the military theory of fortification--with its angles, salients, and bastions--to the topography of the region. The gigantic concrete walls of the bomb-proof shelters, the little forts to shelter the machine guns, and the concrete passages in the rear-line trenches will appear as heavy and massive to future generations as Roman masonry appears to us. There are, of course, many unimportant little links of the trench system, upon whose holding nothing depends and for whose domination neither side cares to spend the life of a single soldier, that have only an apology for a second position. The war needs the money for the preparation of important places. At vital points there may be the tremendously powerful second line, a third line, and even a fourth line. The region between Verdun and the lines, for instance, is the most fearful snarl of barbed wire, pits, and buried explosives that could be imagined. The distance would have to be contested inch by inch.

The trench theory is built about the soldier. It must preserve him as far as possible from artillery and from an infantry attack. The defenses begin with barbed wire; then come the rifles and the machine guns; and behind them the light artillery, the "seventy-fives," and the heavy artillery, the "one hundred and twenties," "two hundred and twenties," and, now, an immense howitzer whose real caliber has been carefully concealed. To take a trench position means the crossing of the entanglements of No Man's Land under fire from artillery, rifles, and machine guns, an almost impossible proceeding. An advance is possible only after the opposing trenches have been made untenable by the concentration of artillery fire. The great offensives begin by blowing the first lines absolutely to pieces; this accomplished, the attacking infantry advances to the vacated trenches under the rifle fire of those few whom the terrible deluge of shells has not killed or crazed, works toward the strong second position under a concentrated artillery fire of the retreating enemy as terrible as its own, fights its way heroically into the second position, and stops there. The great line has been bent, has been dented, but never broken. An offensive must cover at least twenty miles of front, for if the break is too narrow the attacking troops will be massacred by the enemy artillery at both ends of the broken first lines. If the front lines are one mile deep, the artillery must put twenty-five square miles of trenches hors de combat, a task that takes millions of shells. By the time that the first line has been destroyed and the troops have reached the second line, the shells and the men are pretty well used up. A great successful offensive on the western front is theoretically possible, given millions of men, but practically impossible. Outside of important local gains, the great western offensives have been failures. Champagne was a failure, the Calais drive was a failure, Verdun was a failure, and the drive on the Somme has only bent the lines. The Germans may shorten their lines because of a lack of men, but I firmly believe that neither their line nor the Allies' line will ever be broken. What will be the end if the Allies cannot wrest from Germany, Belgium and that part of northern France she is holding for ransom- -to obtain good terms at the peace congress? Is Germany slowly, very slowly going under, or are we going to witness complete European exhaustion? Whatever happens, poor, mourning, desolated France will hold to the end.

In localities where no great offensive is contemplated, and the business of violence has become a routine, the object of the commander is to keep the enemy on the qui-vive, demoralize him by killing and wounding his soldiers, and prevent him from strengthening his first lines. Relations take on the character of an exchange; one day the French throw a thousand mines (high-explosive trench shells) into the German lines, and the next day the Germans throw a thousand back. The French smash up a village where German troops are en repos; while it is being done, the Germans begin to blow a French village to pieces. In the trenches the individual soldiers throw grenades at each other, and wish that the whole tiresome business was done with. They have two weeks in the trenches and two weeks out of them in a cantonment behind the lines. The period in the trenches is divided between the first lines and the rear lines of the first position. Often on my way to the trenches at night I would pass a regiment coming to repos. Silent, vaguely seen, in broken step the regiment passed. Sometimes a shell would come whistling in.

There was one part of the Bois-le-Pretre region upon which nothing depended, and the war had there settled into the casual exchange of powder and old iron that obtains upon two thirds of the front. At the entrance to this position, in the shadow of a beautiful clump of ash trees, stood the rustic shelters of the regimental cooks. From behind the wall of trees came a terrifying crash. The war-gray, iron field kitchen, which the army slang calls a contre-torpilleur (torpedo-boat destroyer), stood in a little clearing of the wood; there was nothing beautiful to the machine, which was simply an iron box, two feet high and four feet square, mounted on big wheels, and fitted with a high oval chimney. A halo of kitcheny smell floated about it, and the open door of its fire-box, in which brands were burning furiously, and a jet of vapor from somewhere, gave it quite the appearance of an odd steam engine. Beside the contre-torpilleur stood the two cooks, both unusually small in stature. One was about thirty-two or three years old, chunky, and gifted with short, strong, hairy arms; the other was much slighter, younger, and so juvenile of face that his downy mustache was almost invisible. I knew these men very well; one, the older, was a farmhand in a village of Touraine, and the other, an errand boy in a bookbinding works at Saint-Denis. The war had turned them into regimental cooks, though it was the older man who did most of the cooking, while the boy occupied himself with gathering wood and distributing the food. The latter once confessed to me that when he heard that Americans were coming to the Bois-le-Pretre, he had expected to see Indians, and that he and his comrades had joked, half in jest, half in earnest, about the Boches going to lose their scalps. The other was famous for an episode of the July attacks: cornered in the trench by a Boche, he had emptied his kettle of hot soup over the man's head and finished him off with a knife. They waved friendlily at me. The farmhand, in particular, was one of the pleasantest fellows who ever breathed; and still fond, like a true good man of Touraine, of a Rabelaisian jest.

The road now entered the wood, and continued straight ahead down a pleasant vista of young ash trees. Suddenly a trench, bearing its name in little black, dauby letters on a piece of yellow board the size of a shingle, began by the side of the forest road, and I went down into it as I might have gone down cellar. The Boyau Poincare--such was its title--began to curve and twist in the manner of trenches, and I came upon a corner in the first line known as "Three Dead Men," because after the capture of the wood, three dead Germans were found there in mysterious, lifelike attitudes. The names of trenches on the French front often reflect that deep, native instinct to poetry possessed by simple peoples--the instinct that created the English ballads and the exquisite mediaeval French legends of the saints. Other trench names were symbolic, or patriotic, or political; we had the "Trench of the Great Revenge," the "Trench of France," the "Trench of Aristide" (meaning Briand), and the "Boulevard Joffre."

Beyond "Les Trois Morts," began the real lines of the position, and as I wound my way through them to the first lines, the pleasant forest of autumnal branches thinned to a wood of trees bare as telegraph poles. It had taken me half an hour to get from the cook's shelters to the first lines, and during that time I had not heard one single explosion. In the first trench the men stood casually by their posts at the parapet, their bluish coats in an interesting contrast to the brown wall of the trench. Behind the sentries, who peered through the rifle slits every once in a while, flowed the usual populace of the first-line trench, passing as casually as if they were on a Parisian sidewalk, officers as miry as their men, poilus of the Engineer Corps with an eye to the state of the rifle boxes, and an old, unshaven soldier in light-brown corduroy trousers and blue jacket, who volunteered the information that the Boches had thrown a grenade at him as he turned the corner "down there"--"It didn't go off." So calm an atmosphere pervaded the cold, sunny, autumnal afternoon that the idea "the trenches" took on the proportions of a gigantic hoax; we might have been masqueraders in the trenches after the war was over. And the Germans were only seventy-five feet away, across those bare poles, stumps, and matted dead brown leaves!

"Attention!"

The atmosphere of the trench changed in a second. Every head in sight looked up searchingly at the sky. Just over the trees, distinctly seen, was a little, black, cylindrical package somersaulting through the air. In another second everybody had calculated the spot in which it was about to land, and those whom it threatened had swiftly found shelter, either by continuing down the trench to a sharp turn, running into the door of an abri (shelter), or simply snuggling into a hole dug in the side of the trench. There was a moment of full, complete silence between the time when everybody had taken refuge and the explosion of the trench shell. The missile burst with that loud hammer pound made by a thick-walled iron shell, and lay smoking in the withered leaves.

"It begins--it begins," said an old poilu, tossing his head. "Now we shall have those pellets all afternoon."

An instant after the burst the trench relaxed; some of the sentries looked back to see where the shell had fallen, others paid no attention to it whatsoever. Once again the quiet was disturbed by a muffled boom somewhere ahead of us, and everybody calculated and took refuge exactly as before. The shells began to come, one on the heels of the other with alarming frequency; hardly had one burst when another was discovered in the air. The poilus, who had taken the first shells as a matter of course, good-naturedly even, began to get as cross as peevish schoolboys. It was decidedly too much of a good thing. Finally the order was given for every one except the sentinels, who were standing under the occasional shelters of beams and earth bridged across the trench, to retire to the abris. I saw one of the exposed sentinels as I withdrew, a big, heavily built, young fellow with a face as placid as that of a farm animal; his rifle leaned against the earth of the trench, and the shadow of the shelter fell on his expressionless features. The next sentinel was a man in the late thirties, a tall, nervous soldier with a fierce, aggressive face.

The abri to which we retired was about twenty-five feet long and eight feet wide, and had a door at either end. The hut had been dug right in the crude, calcareous rock of Lorraine, and the beams of the roof were deeply set into these natural walls. Along the front wall ran a corridor about a foot wide, and between this corridor and the rear wall was a raised platform about seven feet wide piled with hay. Sprawled in this hay, in various attitudes, were about fifteen men, the squad that had just completed its sentry service. Two candles hung from the massive roof and flickered in the draughts between the two doors, revealing, in rare periods of radiance, a shelf along the wall over the sleepers' heads piled with canteens, knapsacks, and helmets. In the middle of the rock wall by the corridor a semicircular funnel had been carved out to serve as a fireplace, and at its base a flameless fire of beautiful, crumbling red brands was glowing. This hearth cut in the living rock was very wonderful and beautiful. Suddenly a trench shell landed right on the roof of the abri, shaking little fragments of stone down into the fire on the hearth. The soldiers, who sat hunched up on the edge of the platform, their feet in the corridor, gave vent to a burst of anger that had its source in exasperation.

"This is going too far."--"Why don't they answer?"--"Are those dirty cows (the classic sales vaches) going to keep this up all afternoon?"

"Really, now, this is getting to be a real nuisance." Suddenly two forms loomed large in the left doorway, and the stolid sentry of whom I have spoken limped in on the arm of an infirmier. Voices murmured in the obscurity, "Who is wounded?"--"Somebody wounded?" And dreamy-eyed ones sat up in the straw. The stolid one--he could not have been much over twenty-one or two--sat down on the edge of the straw near the fireplace, his face showing no emotion, only a pallor. He had a painful but not serious wound; a small fragment of iron, from a shell that had fallen directly into the trench, had lodged in the bones of his foot. He took off his big, ugly shoe and rested the blood-stained sock on the straw. Voices like echoes traveled the length of the shelter--"Is it thou, Jarnac?"--"Art thou wounded, Jarnac?" "Yes," answered the big fellow in a bass whisper. He was a peasant of the Woevre, one of a stolid, laborious race.

"The lieutenant has gone to the telephone shelter to ring up the batteries," said the infirmier. "Good," said a vibrant, masculine voice somewhere in the straw.

A shell coming toward you from the enemy makes a good deal of noise, but it is not to be compared to the noise made by one's own shells rushing on a slant just over one's head to break in the enemy's trenches seventy-five feet away. A swift rafale of some fifty "seventy-five" shells passed whistling like the great wind of the Apocalypse, which is to blow when the firmament collapses. Looking through the rifle slit, after the rafale was over, I could see puffs of smoke apparently rising out of the carpet of dead leaves. The nervous man, the other sentry, held up his finger for us not to make the slightest noise and whispered,--

"I heard somebody yell."

"Where?"

"Over there by that stump."

We strained our ears to catch a sound, but heard nothing.

"I heard the yell plainly," replied the sentry.

The news seemed to give some satisfaction. At any rate, the Germans stopped their trench shells. The quiet hush of late afternoon was at hand. Soon the cook came down the trench with kettles of hot soup.

Five months have passed since I last saw the inhabitants of this abri, the tenants of the "Ritz-Marmite." How many are still alive? What has happened to this fine, brave crowd of Frenchmen, gentlemen all, bons camarades? I have seen them on guard in a heavy winter snowstorm, when the enemy was throwing grenades which, exploding, blew purplish-black smudges on the snow; I have seen them so bemired in mud and slop that they looked like effigies of brownish earth; I have watched them wading through communication trenches that were veritable canals. And this is the third year of the war.

The most interesting of the lot mentally was a young Socialist named Hippolyte. He was a sous-lieutenant of the Engineers, and had quarters of his own in the rear of the trenches, where one was always sure to find books on social questions lying round in the hay. When the war began he was just finishing his law course at the University of Montpellier. A true son of the South, he was dark, short, but well proportioned, with small hands and feet. The distinguishing features of his countenance were his eyes and mouth--the eyes, eloquent, alert, almost Italian; the mouth, full, firm, and dogmatic. The great orators of the Midi must have resembled him in their youth. He was a Socialist and a pacifist a outrance, continuing his dream of universal fraternity in the midst of war. His work lay in building a tunnel under the Germans, by which he hoped to blow part of the German trenches, Teutons and all, sky-high.

The tunnei (sape) began in the third line, at a door hi the wall of the trench strongly framed in wooden beams the size of railroad ties. At occasional intervals along the passage the roof was reinforced by a frame of these beams, so that the sape had the businesslike, professional look of a gallery in a coal mine. Descending steeply to a point twelve feet beyond the entrance, it then went at a gentle incline under No Man's Land, and ended beneath the German trenches. It was the original intention to blow up part of the German first line, but it being one day discovered that the Germans were building a tunnel parallel to the French one, it was decided to blow up the French safe so that the explosion would spend its force underground, and cause the walls of the German tunnel to cave in on its makers. I happened to see the tunnel the morning of the day it was blown up. The French had stopped working for fear of being overheard by the Germans. It was a ticklish situation. Were the

Germans aware of the French tunnel? If so, they would blow up their own at once. Were they still continuing their labor? The earth of the French might burst apart anyminute and rain down again in a dreadful shower of clods, stones, and mangled bodies.

Alone, quiet, at the end of the passage under the German lines sat an old poilu, the sentinel of the tunnel. He was an old coal miner of the North. The light of a candle showed his quiet, bearded face, grave as the countenance of some sculptured saint on the portico of a Gothic church, and revealed the wrinkles and lines of many years of labor. The sentinel held a microphone to his ears; the poles of it disappearing into the wall of damp earth separating us from the Boches.

Hippolyte whispered, "You hear them?"

The old man nodded his head, and gave the microphone to his officer. I saw Hippolyte listen. Then, without a word, he handed it to me. All that I could hear was a faint tapping.

"The Boches," whispered Hippolyte.

The French blew up the sape early in the afternoon, at a time when they felt sure the Germans were at work in their tunnel. I saw the result the next day. A saucer-shaped depression about twenty-five feet in diameter, and perhaps two feet deep, had appeared in No Man's Land. Even the stumps of two trees had sunk and tilted.

It was Hippolyte who had turned on the electricity. I once talked the matter over with him. He became at once intense, Latin, doctrinaire.

"How do you reconcile your theories of fraternity to what you have to do?"

"I do not have to reconcile my theories to my office; I am furthering my theories."

"How so?"

"By combating the Boches. Without them we might have realized our idea of universal peace and fraternity. Voila l'ennemi! The race is a poisonous race, serpents, massacreurs! I wish I could smother as many of them every day as I did yesterday."

During my service I did not meet another soldier whose hatred of the Germans was comparable to that of this advocate of universal love.

I left the trenches just at dusk. Above the dreadful depression in No Man's Land shone a bronzy sky against which the trees raised their haggard silhouettes. There was hardly a sound in the whole length of The Wood. A mist came up making haloes round the rising winter stars.

Chapter VI
The Germans Attack

The schoolmaster (instituteur) and the schoolmistress (institutrice) of Montauville were a married couple, and had a flat of four rooms on the second story of the schoolhouse. The kitchen of this fiat had been struck by a shell, and was still a mess of plaster, bits of stone, and glass, and a fragment had torn clear through the sooty bottom of a copper saucepan still hanging on the wall. In one of the rooms, else quite bare of furniture, was an upright piano. Sometimes while stationed at Montauville, I whiled away the waits between calls to the trenches in playing this instrument.

It was about nine o'clock in the morning, and thus far not a single call had come in. The sun was shining very brightly in a sky washed clear by a night of rain, the morning mists were rising from the wood, and up and down the very muddy street walked little groups of soldiers. I drew up the rickety stool and began to play the waltz from "The Count of Luxembourg." In a short time I heard the sound of tramping on the stairs voices. In came three poilus--a pale boy with a weary, gentle expression in his rather faded blue eyes; a dark, heavy fellow of twenty-five or six, with big wrists, big, muscular hands, and a rather unpleasant, lowering face; and a little, middle-aged man with straightforward, friendly hazel eyes and a pointed beard. The pale, boyish one carried a violin made from a cigar box under his arm, just such a violin as the darkies make down South. This violin was very beautifully made, and decorated with a rustic design. I stopped playing.

"Don't, don't," cried the dark, big fellow; "we haven't heard any music for a long time. Please keep on. Jacques, here, will accompany you."

"I never heard the waltz," said the violinist; "but if you play it over for me once or twice, I'll try to get the air--if you would like to have me to," he added with a shy, gentle courtesy.

So I played the rather banal waltz again, till the lad caught the tune. He hit it amazingly well, and his ear was unusually true. The dark one had been in Canada and was hungry for American rag-time. "'The Good Old Summer Time'--you know that? 'Harrigan'--you know that?" he said in English. The rag-time of "Harrigan" floated out on the street of Montauville. But I did not care to play things which could have no violin obligato, so I began to play what I remembered of waltzes dear to every Frenchman's heart--the tunes of the "Merry Widow." "Sylvia" went off with quite a dash. The concert was getting popular. Somebody wanted to send for a certain Alphonse who had an occarina. Two other poilus, men in the forties, came up, their dark-brown, horseshoe beards making them look like brothers. Side by side against the faded paper on the sunny wall they stood, surveying us contentedly. The violinist, who turned out to be a Norman, played a solo--some music-hall fantasy, I imagine. The next number was the ever popular "Tipperaree," which every single poilu in the French army has learned to sing in a kind of English. Our piano-violin duet hit off this piece even better than the "Merry Widow." I thanked Heaven that I was not called on to translate it, a feat frequently demanded of the American drivers. The song is silly enough in the King's English, but in lucid, exact French, it sinks to positive imbecility.

"You play, don't you?" said the violinist to the small bearded man.

"A little," he replied modestly.

"Please play."

The little man sat down at the piano, meditated a minute, and began to play the rich chords of Rachmaninof's "Prelude." He got about half through, when Zip-bang! a small shell burst down the street. The dark fellow threw open the French window. The poilus were scurrying to shelter. The pianist continued with the "Prelude."

Zip-bang! Zip-bang! Zshh--Bang--Bang. Bang-Bang!

The piano stopped. Everybody listened. The village was still as death. Suddenly down the street came the rattle of a volley of rifle shots. Over this sound rose the choked, metallic notes of a bugle-call. The rifle shots continued. The ominous popping of machine guns resounded. The village, recovering from its silence, filled with murmurs. Bang! Bang! Bang I Bang! went some more shells. The same knowledge took definite shape in our minds.

"An attack!"

The violinist, clutching his instrument, hurried down the stairs followed by all the others, leaving the chords of the uncompleted "Prelude" to hang in the startled air. Shells were popping everywhere--crashes of smoke and violence--in the roads, in the fields, and overhead. The Germans were trying to isolate the few detachments en repos in the village, and prevent reinforcements coming from Dieulouard or any other place. To this end all the roads between Pont-a-Mousson and the trenches, and the roads leading directly to the trenches, were being shelled.

"Go at once to Poste C!"

The winding road lay straight ahead, and just at the end of the village street, the Germans had established a tir de barrage. This meant that a shell was falling at that particular point about once every fifty seconds. I heard two rafales break there as I was grinding up the machine. Up the slope of the Montauville hill came several of the other drivers. Tyler, of New York, a comrade who united remarkable bravery to the kindest of hearts, followed close behind me, also evidently bound for Poste C. German bullets, fired wildly from the ridge of The Wood over the French trenches, sang across the Montauville valley, lodging in the trees of Puvenelle behind us with a vicious tspt; shells broke here and there on the stretch leading to the Quart-en-Reserve, throwing the small rocks of the road surfacing wildly in every direction. The French batteries to our left were firing at the Germans, the German batteries were firing at the French trenches and the roads, and the machine guns rattled ceaselessly. I saw the poilus hurrying up the muddy roads of the slope of the Bois-le-Pretre--vague masses of moving blue on the brown ways. A storm of shells was breaking round certain points in the road and particularly at the entrance to The Wood. I wondered what had become of the audience at the concert. Various sounds, transit of shells, bursting of shells, crashing of near-by cannon, and rat-tat-tat-tat! of mitrailleuses played the treble to a roar formed of echoes and cadences--the roar of battle. The Wood of Death (Le Bois de la Mort) was singing again.

That day's attack was an attempt by the Germans to take back from the French the eastern third of the Quart-en-Reserve and the rest of the adjoining ridge half hidden in the shattered trees. At the top of the plateau, by the rise in the moorland I described in the preceding chapter, I had an instant's view of the near-by battle, for the focus was hardly more than four hundred yards away. There was a glimpse of human beings in the Quart--soldiers in green, soldiers in blue--the very fact that anybody was to be seen there was profoundly stirring. They were fighting in No Man's Land. Tyler and I watched for a second, wondering what scenes of agony, of heroism, of despair were being enacted in that dreadful field by the ruined wood.

We hurried our wounded to the hospital, passing on our way detachments of soldiers rushing toward The Wood from the villages of the region. Three or four big shells had just fallen in Dieulouard, and the village was deserted and horribly still. The wind carried the roar of the attack to our ears. In three quarters of an hour, I was back again at the same moorland poste, to which an order of our commander had attached me. Montauville was full of wounded. I had three on stretchers inside, one beside me on the seat, and two others on the front mudguards. And The Wood continued to sing. From Montauville I could hear the savage yells and cries which accompanied the fighting.

Half an hour after the beginning of the attack, the war invaded the sky, with the coming of the German reconnoitering aeroplanes. One went to watch the roads leading to The Wood along the plateau, one went to watch the Dieulouard road, and the other hovered over the scene of the combat. The sky was soon dotted with the puffs of smoke left by the exploding shells of the special anti-aircraft "seventy-fives." These puffs blossomed from a pin-point of light to a vaporous, gray-white puff-ball about the size of the full moon, and then dissolved in the air or blew about in streaks and wisps. These cloudlets, fired at an aviator flying along a certain line, often were gathered by the eye into arrangements resembling constellations. The three machines were very high, and had a likeness to little brown and silver insects.

The Boche watching the conflict appeared to hang almost immobile over the Quart. With a striking suddenness, another machine appeared behind him and above him. So unexpected was the approach of this second aeroplane that its appearance had a touch of the miraculous. It might have been created at that very moment in the sky. The Frenchman--for it was an aviator from the parc at Toul, since killed at Verdun, poor fellow--swooped beneath his antagonist and fired his machine gun at him. The German answered with two shots of a carbine. The Frenchman fired again. Suddenly the German machine flopped to the right and swooped down; it then flopped to the left, the tail of the machine flew up, and the apparatus fell, not so swiftly as one might expect, down a thousand feet into The Wood. When I saw the wreckage, a few days afterwards, it looked like the spilt contents of a waste-paper basket, and the aviators, a pilot and an observer, had had to be collected from all over the landscape. The French buried them with full military honors.

Thanks to the use of a flame machine, the Germans succeeded in regaining the part of the ridge they had lost, but the French made it so hot for them that they abandoned it, and the contested trenches now lie in No Man's Land. All that night the whole Wood was illuminated, trench light after trench light rising over the dark branches. There would be a rocket like the trail of bronze-red powder sparks hanging for an instant in the sky, then a loud Plop! and the French light would spread out its parachute and sail slowly down the sky toward the river. The German lights (fusees eclairantes), cartridges of magnesium fired from a gun resembling a shotgun, burned only during their dazzling trajectory. At midnight the sky darkened with low, black rain clouds, upon whose surface the constant cannon fire flashed in pools of violet-white light. Coming down from the plateau at two in the morning, I could see sharp jabs of cannon fire for thirty miles along the front on the other side of the Moselle.

Just after this attack a doctor of the army service was walking through the trenches in which the French had made their stand. He noticed something oddly skewered to a tree. He knocked it down with a stone, and a human heart fell at his feet.

The most interesting question of the whole business is, "How do the soldiers stand it?" At the beginning of my own service, I thought Pont-a-Mousson, with its ruins, its danger, and its darkness, the most awful place on the face of the earth. After a little while, I grew accustomed to the decor, and when the time came for me to leave it, I went with as much regret as if I were leaving the friendliest, most peaceful of towns. First the decor, growing familiar, lost the keener edges of its horror, and then the life of the front--the violence, the destruction, the dying and the dead--all became casual, part of the day's work. A human being is profoundly affected by those about him; thus, when a new soldier finds himself for the first time in a trench, he is sustained by the attitude of the veterans. Violence becomes the commonplace; shells, gases, and flames are the things that life is made of. The war is another lesson in the power of the species to adapt itself to circumstances. When this power of adaptability has been reinforced by a tenacious national will "to see the thing through," men will stand hell itself. The slow, dogged determination of the British cannot be more powerful than the resolution of the French. Their decision to continue at all costs has been reached by a purely intellectual process, and to enforce it, they have called upon those ancient foundations of the French character, the sober reasonableness and unbending will they inherit from Rome.

And a new religion has risen in the trenches, a faith much more akin to Mahomet than to Christ. It is a fatalism of action. The soldier finds his salvation in the belief that nothing will happen to him until his hour comes, and the logical corollary of this belief, that it does no good to worry, is his rock of ages. It is a curious thing to see poilus--peasants, artisans, scholars--completely in the grip of this philosophy. There has been a certain return to the Church of Rome, for which several reasons exist, the greatest being that the war has made men turn to spiritual things. Only an animal could be confronted with the pageant of heroism, the glory of sacrifice, and the presence of Death, and not be moved to a contemplation of the fountain-head of these sublime mysteries. But it is the upper class which in particular has returned to the Church. Before the war, rationalist and genial skeptic, the educated Frenchman went to church because it was the thing to do, and because non-attendance would weaken an institution which the world was by no means ready to lay aside. This same educated Frenchman, brought face to face with the mystery of human existence, has felt a real need of spiritual support, and consequently returned to the Church of his fathers.

The religious revival is a return of upper-class prodigals to the fold, and a rekindling of the chilled brands of the faith of the amiably skeptical. The great mass of the nation has felt this spiritual force, but because the mass of the nation was always Catholic, nothing much has changed. I failed to find any trace of conversions among the still hostile working men of the towns, and the bred-in-the-bone Socialists. The rallying of the conservative classes about the Cross is also due to the fact that the war has exposed the mediocrity and sterile windiness of the old socialistic governments; this misgovernment the upper classes have determined to end once they return from the trenches, and remembering that the Church of Rome was the enemy of the past administrations, cannot help regarding her with a certain friendliness. But this issue of past misgovernment will be fought out on purely secular grounds, and the Church will be only a sympathizer behind the fray. The manner in which the French priests have fought and died is worthy of the admiration of the world. Never in the history of any country has the national religion been so closely enmeshed in the national life. The older clergy, as a rule, have been attached to the medical services of the front, serving as hospital orderlies and stretcher-bearers, but the younger priests have been put right into the army and are fighting to-day as common soldiers. There are hundreds of officer-priests--captains and lieutenants of the regular army.

But the real religion of the front is the philosophy of Mahomet. Life will end only when Death has been decreed by Fate, and the Boches are the unbelievers. After all, Islam in its great days was a virile faith, the faith of a race of soldiers.

Chapter VII
The Town In The Trenches

At the beginning of the war the German plan of campaign was to take France on the flank by marching through Belgium, and once the success of this northern venture assured, strike at the Verdun-Belfort line which had baffled them in the first instance. Had they not lost the battle of the Marne, this second venture might have proved successful, for the body of the French army was fighting in the north, and the remaining troops would have been discouraged by the capture of Paris. On the eve of the battle of the Marne the campaign seeming to be well in hand in the north, a German invasion of Lorraine began, one army striking at the defenses of the great plateau which slopes from the Vosges to the Moselle, and the other attempting to ascend the valley of the river. It was this second army which entered Pont-a-Mousson.

Immediately following the declaration of hostilities the troops who had been quartered in the town were withdrawn, and the town was left open to the enemy who, going very cautiously, was on his way from Metz. For several weeks in August, this city, almost directly on the frontier, saw no soldiers, French or German. It was a time of dramatic suspense. The best recital of it I ever heard came from the lips of the housekeeper of Wisteria Villa, a splendid, brave French woman who had never left her post. She was short, of a clear, tanned complexion, and always had her hair tightly rolled up in a little classic pug. She was as fearless of shells as a soldier in the trenches, and once went to a deserted orchard, practically in the trenches, to get some apples for Messieurs les Americains. When asked why she did not get them at a safer place, she replied that she did not have to pay for these apples as the land belonged to her father! Her ear for shells was the most accurate of the neighborhood, and when a deafening crash would shake the kettles on the stove and rattle the teacups, she could tell you exactly from what direction it had come and the probable caliber. I remember one morning seeing her wash dishes while the Germans were shelling the corner I have already described. The window over the sink opened directly on the dangerous area, and she might have been killed any minute by a flying eclat. Standing with her hands in the soapy water, or wiping dry the hideous blue-and-white dinner service of Wisteria Villa, she never even bothered to look up to see where the shells were landing. Two "seventy-sevens" went off with a horrid pop; "Those are only 'seventy-sevens,'" she murmured as if to herself. A fearful swish was next heard and the house rocked to the din of an explosion. "That's a 'two hundred and ten'--the rogues--oh, the rogues!" she exclaimed in the tone she might have used in scolding a depraved boy.

At night, when the kitchen was cleared up, she sat down to write her daily letter to her soldier son, and once this duty finished, liked nothing better than a friendly chat. She knew the history of Pont-a-Mousson and Montauville and the inhabitants thereof by heart; she had tales to tell of the shrewdness of the peasants and diverting anecdotes of their manners and morals. These stories she told very well and picturesquely.

"The first thing we saw was the President's poster saying not to be alarmed, that the measures of military preparation were required by circumstances (les evenements) and did not mean war. Then over this bill the maire posted a notice that in case of a real mobilization (une mobilisation serieuse) they would ring the tocsin. At eleven o'clock the tocsin rang, oh, la la, monsieur, what a fracas! All the bells in the town, Saint-Martin, Saint-Laurent, the hotel de ville. Immediately all our troops went away. We did not want to see them go. 'We shall be back again,' they said. They liked Pont-a-Mousson. Such good young fellows! The butcher's wife has heard that only fifty-five of the six hundred who were here are alive. They were of the active forces (de l'active). A great many people followed the soldiers. So for two weeks we were left all alone, wondering what was to become of us. And all the time we heard frightful stories about the villages beyond Nancy. On the nth of August we heard cannon for the first time, and on the 12th and the 14th we were bombarded. On the 4th of September, at five o'clock in the evening, the bells began to ring again. Everybody ran out to find the reason. Les Allemands--they were not then called Boches--were coming. Baoum! went the bridge over the Moselle. Everybody went into their houses, so that the Germans came down streets absolutely deserted. I peeked from my window blind. The Boches came down the road from Norroy, les Uhlans, the infantry--how big and ugly they all were. And their officers were so stiff (raide). They were not like our bons petits soldats Francais. In the morning I went out to get some bread.

"'Eh la, good woman' (bonne femme), said a grand Boche to me.

"'What do you want?' said I.

"'Are there any soldats francais in the town?' said the Boche.

"'How should I know?' I answered.

"'You do not want to tell, good woman.'

"'I do not know.'

"'Are there any francs-tireurs (civilian snipers) in this town?'

"'Don't bother me; I'm going for some bread.'

"During the night all the clocks had been changed to German time. Many of the Boches spoke French. There were Alsatians and Lorrains who did not like the fracas at all. Yes, the Boches behaved themselves all right at Pont-a-Mousson--there were some vulgarities (grossieretes). One of the soldiers, a big blond, went down the street wearing an ostrich feather hat and a woman's union suit and chemise. It was a scandale. But uncle laughed to kill himself; he was peeping out through the blinds. Right in front of my door were ten cannon, and all the street was full of artillery. Well we had four days of this, hearing never a word from the French side.

"On the night of the 9th I heard a good deal of noise, and somebody woke up the Boches sous-officiers who were quartered in a house across the street. I saw lights and heard shouts. I was peeping out of my window all the time. The dark street filled with soldiers. I saw their officers lashing them to make them hurry. They harnessed the artillery horses to the guns, and at four o'clock in the morning there was not a single Boche in Pont-a-Mousson. They had all gone away in the night, taking with them the German flag on the city hall. You know, monsieur, on the night of the 9th they received news of the battle of the Marne.

"For five days more we saw neither Francais nor Boches. Finally some French dragoons came down the road from Dieulouard, and little by little other soldiers came too. But, helas, monsieur, the Boches were waiting for them in the Bois-le-Pretre."

Such was the way that Pont-a-Mousson did not become Mussenbruck. The episode is an agreeable interlude of decency in the history of German occupations, for that atrocities were perpetrated in Nomeny, just across the river, is beyond question. I have talked with survivors. At Pont-a-Mousson everything was orderly; six miles to the east, houses were burned over the heads of the inhabitants, and women and children brutally massacred.

I best remember the little city as it was one afternoon in early December. The population of 17,000 had then shrunk to about 900, and only a little furtive life lingered in the town. My promenade began at the river-bank by the wooden footbridge crossing from the shore to the remaining arches of the graceful eighteenth-century stone bridge blown up in September, 1914. There is always something melancholy about a ruined bridge, perhaps because the structure symbolizes a patient human victory over the material world. There was something intensely tragic in the view of the wrecked quarter of Saint-Martin, seen across the deep, greenish, wintry river, and in the great curve of the broad flood sullenly hurrying to Metz. At the end of the bridge, ancient and gray, rose the two round towers of the fifteenth-century parish church, with that blind, solemn look to them the towers of Notre Dame possess, and beyond this edifice, a tile-roofed town and the great triangular hill called the Mousson. It was dangerous to cross the bridge, because German snipers occasionally fired at it, so I contented myself with looking down the river. Beyond the Bois-le-Pretre, the next ridge to rise from the river was a grassy spur bearing the village of Norroy on its back. You could see the hill, only four kilometres away, the brown walls of the village, the red roofs, and sometimes the glint of sunlight on a window; but for us the village might have been on another planet. All social and economic relations with Norroy had ceased since September, 1914, and reflecting on this fact, the invisible wall of the trenches became more than a mere military wall, became a barrier to every human relation and peaceful tie.

A sentry stood by the ruined bridge, a small, well-knit man with beautiful silver-gray hair, blue eyes, and pink cheeks; his uniform was exceptionally clean, and he appeared to be some decent burgher torn from his customary life. I fell into conversation with him. He recollected that his father, a veteran of 1870, had prophesied the present war.

"'We shall see them again, the spiked helmets (les casques a pointe),' said my father--'we shall see them again.'

"'Why?' I asked him.

"'Because they have eaten of us, and will be hungry once more.'"

The principal street of the town led from this bridge to a great square, and continued straight on toward Maidieres and Montauville. The sidewalks around this square were in arcades under the houses, for the second story of every building projected for seven or eight feet over the first and rested on a line of arches at the edge of the street. To avoid damage from shells bursting in the open space, every one of these arcades, and there were perhaps a hundred all told, had been plugged with sandbags, so that the square had an odd, blind look. A little life flickered in the damp, dark alleys behind these obstructions. There was a tobacco shop, kept by two pretty young women whom the younger soldiers were always jollying, a wineshop, a tailorshop, and a bookstore, always well supplied with the great Parisian weeklies, which one found later in odd corners of shelters in the trenches. Occasionally a soldier bought a serious book when it was to be found in the dusty files of the "Collection Nelson"; I remember seeing a young lieutenant of artillery buying Segur's "Histoire de la Grande Armee en 1812," and another taking Flaubert's "Un coeur simple." But the military life, roughly lived, and shared with simple people, appears to make even the wisest boyish, and after a while at the front the intellect will not read anything intellectual. It simply won't, perhaps because it can't. The soldier mind delights in rough, genial, and simple jokes. A sergeant, whom I knew to be a distinguished young scholar in civilian life, was always throwing messages wrapped round a stone into the German trenches; the messages were killingly funny, amiably indecent, and very jejune. Invariably they provoked a storm of grenades, and sometimes epistles in the same vein from the Boches. In spite of the vicious pang of the grenades, there was an absurd "Boys-will-be-boys" air to the whole performance. Conversation, however, did not sink to this boyish level, and the rag-tag and bob-tail of one's cultivation found its outlet in speech.

At the end of this street was the railroad crossing, the passage a niveau, and the station in a jungle of dead grass and brambles. Like the bridge, its rustiness and weediness was a dreadful symbol of the cessation of human activity, and the blue enamel signpost lettered in white with the legend, "Metz--32 kilometres," was another reminder of the town to which the French aspired with all the fierce intensity of crusaders longing for Jerusalem. It was impossible to get away from the omnipresence of the name of the fated city--it stared at you from obscure street corners, and was to be found on the covers of printed books and post-cards. I saw the city once from the top of the hill of the Mousson; its cathedral towers pierced the blue mists of the brown moorlands, and it appeared phantasmal and tremendously distant. Yet for those towers countless men had died, were dying, would die. A French soldier who had made the ascent with me pointed out Metz the much desired.

"Are you going to get it?" I asked. "Perhaps so," he replied gravely. "After so many sacrifices." (Apres tant de sacrifices.) He made no gesture, but I know that his vision included the soldiers' cemetery at the foot of the Mousson hill. It lay, a rust-colored field, on the steep hillside just at the border of the town, and was new, raw, and dreadful. The guardian of the cemetery, an old veteran of 1870, once took me through the place. He was a very lean, hooped-over old man with a big, aquiline nose, blue-gray eyes framed in red lids, and a huge, yellowish-white mustache. First he showed me the hideous picture of the civilian cemetery, in which giant shells had torn open the tombs, hurled great sarcophagi a distance of fifty feet, and dug craters in the rows of graves. Though the civilian authorities had done what they could to put the place in order, there were still memories of the disturbed dead to whom the war had denied rest. Coming to the military cemetery, the guardian whispered, pointing to the new mounds with his rustic cane, "I have two colonels, three commandants, and a captain. Yes, two colonels" (deux colonels). Following his staff, my eye looked at the graves as if it expected to see the living men or their effigies. Somewhat apart lay another grave. "Voila un colonel boche," said the sexton; "and a lieutenant boche--and fifty soldats boches."

The destroyed quarter of Pont-a-Mousson lay between the main street and the flank of the Bois-le-Pretre. The quarter was almost totally deserted, probably not more than ten houses being inhabited out of several thousand. The streets that led into it had grass growing high in the gutters, and a velvety moss wearing a winter rustiness grew packed between the paving-stones. Beyond the main street, la rue Fabvrier went straight down this loneliness, and halted or turned at a clump of wrecked houses a quarter of a mile away. Over this clump, slately-purple and cold, appeared the Bois-le-Pretre, and every once in a while a puffy cloud of greenish-brown or gray-black would float solemnly over the crests of the trees. This stretch of la rue Fabvrier was one of the most melancholy pictures it was possible to see. Hardly a house had been spared by the German shells; there were pock-marks and pits of shell fragments in the plaster, window glass outside, and holes in walls and roofs. I wandered down the street, passing the famous miraculous statue of the Virgin of Pont-a-Mousson. The image, only a foot or two high and quite devoid of facial expression, managed somehow to express emotion in the outstretched arms, drooping in a gesture at once of invitation and acceptance. A shell had maculated the wall on each side and above the statue, but the little niche and canopy were quite untouched. The heavy sound of my soldier boots went dump! clump! down the silence.

At the end of the road, in the fields on the slope, a beautiful eighteenth-century house stood behind a mossy green wall. It was just such a French house as is the analogue of our brick mansions of Georgian days; it was two stories high and had a great front room on each side of an entry on both floors, each room being light-ed with two well-proportioned French windows. The outer walls were a golden brown, and the roof, which curved in gently from the four sides to central ridge, a very beautiful rich red. The house had the atmosphere of the era of the French Revolution; one's fancy could people it with soberly dressed provincial grandees. A pare of larches and hemlocks lay about it, concealing in their silent obscurity an artificial lake heavily coated with a pea-soup scum.

Beyond the house lay the deserted rose-garden, rank and grown to weeds. On some of the bushes were cankered, frozen buds. In the center of the garden, at the meeting-point of several paths, a mossy fountain was flowing into a greenish basin shaped like a seashell, and in this basin a poilu was washing his clothes. He was a man of thirty-eight or nine, big, muscular, out-of-doors looking; whistling, he washed his gray underclothes with the soap the army furnishes, wrung them, and tossed them over the rose-bushes to dry.

"Does anybody live in this house?"

"Yes, a squad of travailleurs."

A regiment of travailleurs is attached to every secteur of trenches. These soldiers, depending, I believe, on the Engineer Corps, are quartered just behind the lines, and go to them every day to put them in order, repair the roads, and do all the manual labor. Humble folk these, peasants, ditch-diggers, road-menders, and village carpenters. Those at Pont-a-Mousson were nearly all fathers of families, and it was one of the sights of the war most charged with true pathos to see these gray-haired men marching to the trenches with their shovels on their shoulders.

"Are you comfortable?"

"Oh, yes. We live very quietly. I, being a stonemason and a carpenter, stay behind and keep the house in repair. In summer we have our little vegetable gardens down behind those trees where the Boches can't see us."

"Can I see the house?"

"Surely; just wait till I have finished sousing these clothes."

The room on the ground floor to the left of the hallway was imposing in a stately Old-World way. The rooms in Wisteria Villa were rooms for personages from Zola; this room was inhabited by ghosts from the pages of Balzac. It was large, high, and square; the walls were hung with a golden scroll design printed on ancient yellow silk; the furniture was of some rich brown finish with streaks and lusters of bronzy yellow, and a glass chandelier, all spangles and teardrops of crystal, hung from a round golden panel in the ceiling. Over a severe Louis XVI mantel was a large oil portrait of Pius IX, and on the opposite wall a portrait head of a very beautiful young girl. Chestnut hair, parted in the fashion of the late sixties, formed a silky frame round an oval face, and the features were small and well proportioned. The most remarkable part of the countenance were the curiously level eyes. The calm, apart-from-the-world character of the expression in the eyes was in interesting contrast to the good-natured and somewhat childish look in the eyes of the old Pope.

"Who lived here?"

"An old man (un vieux). He was a captain of the Papal Zouaves in his youth. See here, read the inscription on the portrait--'Presented by His Holiness to a champion (defenseur) of the Church.'"

"Is he still alive?"

"He died three months ago in Paris. I should hate to die before I see how the war is going to end. I imagine he would have been willing to last a bit longer."

"And this picture on the right, the jeune fille?"

"That was his daughter, an only child. She became a nun, and died when she was still young. The old man's gardener comes round from time to time to see if the place is all right. It is a pity he is not here; he could tell you all about them."

"You are very fortunate not to have been blown to pieces. Surely you are very near the trenches."

"Near enough--yes, indeed. A communication trench comes right into the cellar. But it is quiet in this part of The Wood. There is a regiment of old Boches in the trenches opposite our territorials, fathers of families (peres de familles), just as they are. We fire rifles at each other from time to time just to remember it is war (c'est la guerre). We share the crest together here; nothing depends on it. What good should we do in killing each other? Besides it would be a waste of shells."

"How do you know that the Boches opposite you are old?"

"We see them from time to time. They are great hands at a parley. The first thing they tell you is the number of children they have. I met an old Boche not long ago down by the river. He held up two fingers to show that he had two children, put his hand out just above his knee to show the height of his first child, and raised it just above his waist to show the height of the second. So I held up five fingers to show him I had five children, when the Lord knows I have only one. But I did not want to be beaten by a Boche."

A sound of voices was heard beneath us, and the clang of the shovels being placed against the stone walls of the cellar.

"Those are the travailleurs. The sergeant will be coming in and I must report to him. Good-bye, American friend, and come again."

A melancholy dusk was beginning as I turned home from the romantic house, and the deserted streets were filling with purplish shadows. The concussion of exploding shells had blown almost all the glass out of the windows of the Church of St. Laurent, and the few brilliant red and yellow fragments that still clung to the twisted leaden frames reminded me of the autumn leaves that sometimes cling to winter-stricken trees. The interior of the church was swept and garnished, and about twenty candles with golden flames, slowly waving in the drafts from the ruined windows, shone beneath a statue of the Virgin. There was not another soul in the church. A terrible silence fell with the gathering darkness. In a little wicker basket at the foot of the benignant mother were about twenty photographs of soldiers, some in little brassy frames with spots of verdigris on them, some the old-fashioned "cabinet" kind, some on simple post-cards. There was a young, dark Zouave who stood with his hand on an ugly little table, a sergeant of the Engineer Corps with a vacant, uninteresting face, and two young infantry men, brothers, on the same shabby finger-marked post-card. Pious hands had left them thus in the care of the unhappy mother, "Marie, consolatrice des malheureux."

The darkness of midnight was beginning at Pont-a-Mousson, for the town was always as black as a pit. On my way home I saw a furtive knife edge of yellow light here and there under a door. The sentry stood by his shuttered lantern. Suddenly the first of the trench lights flowered in the sky over the long dark ridge of the Bois-le-Pretre.

Chapter VIII
Messieurs Les Poilus De La Grande Guerre

The word "poilu," now applied to a French soldier, means literally "a hairy one," but the term is understood metaphorically. Since time immemorial the possession of plenty of bodily hair has served to indicate a certain sturdy, male bearishness, and thus the French, long before the war, called any good, powerful fellow--"un veritable poilu." The term has been found applied to soldiers of the Napoleonic wars. The French soldier of to-day, coming from the trenches looking like a well-digger, but contented, hearty, and strong, is the poilu par excellence.

The origin of the term "Boche," meaning a German, has been treated in a thousand articles, and controversy has raged over it. The probable origin of the term, however, lies in the Parisian slang word "caboche," meaning an ugly head. This became shortened to "Boche," and was applied to foreigners of Germanic origin, in exactly the way that the American-born laborer applies the contemptuous term "square-head" to his competitors from northern Europe. The word "Boche" cannot be translated by anything except "Boche," any more than our word "Wop," meaning an Italian, can be turned into French. The same attitude, half banter, half race contempt, lies at the heart of both terms.

When the poilus have faced the Boches for two weeks in the trenches, they march down late at night to a village behind the lines, far enough away from the batteries to be out of danger of everything except occasional big shells, and near enough to be rushed up to the front in case of an attack. There they are quartered in houses, barns, sheds, and cellars, in everything that can decently house and shelter a man. These two weeks of repos are the poilus' elysium, for they mean rest from strain, safety, and comparative comfort. The English have behind their lines model villages with macadam roads, concrete sidewalks, a water system, a sewer system, and all kinds of schemes to make the soldiers happy; the French have to be contented with an ordinary Lorraine village, kept in good order by the Medical Corps, but quite destitute of anything as chic as the British possess.

The village of cantonnement is pretty sure to be the usual brown-walled, red-roofed village of Lorraine clumped round its parish church or mouldering castle. In such a French village there is always a hall, usually over the largest wineshop, called the "Salle de Fetes," and this hall serves for the concert each regiment gives while en repos. The Government provides for, indeed insists upon, a weekly bath, and the bathhouse, usually some converted factory or large shed, receives its daily consignments of companies, marching up to the douches as solemnly as if they were going to church. Round the army continues the often busy life of the village, for to many such a hamlet the presence of a multitude of soldiers is a great economic boon. Grocery-shops, in particular, do a rushing business, for any soldier who has a sou is glad to vary the government menu with such delicacies as pates de foie gras, little sugar biscuits, and the well- beloved tablet of chocolate.

While the grocery-man (l'epicier) is fighting somewhere in the north or in the Argonne, madame l'epiciere stays at home and serves the customers. At her side is her own father, an old fellow wearing big yellow sabots, and perhaps the grocer's son and heir, a boy about twelve years old. Madame is dressed entirely in black, not because she is in mourning, but because it is the rural fashion; she wears a knitted shoulder cape, a high black collar, and moves in a brisk, businesslike way; the two men wear the blue-check overalls persons of their calling affect, in company with very clean white collars and rather dirty, frayed bow ties of unlovely patterns. Along the counter stand the poilus, young, old, small, and large, all wearing various fadings of the horizon blue, and helmets often dented. "Some pate de foie gras, madame, s'il vous plait." "Oui, monsieur." "How much is this cheese, maman?" cries the boy in a shrill treble. In the barrel-haunted darkness at the rear of the shop, the old man fumbles round for some tins of jelly. The poilu is very fond of sweets. Sometimes swish bang! a big shell comes in unexpectedly, and shopkeepers and clients hurry, at a decent tempo, to the cellar. There, in the earthy obscurity, one sits down on empty herring-boxes and vegetable cases to wait calmly for the exasperating Boches to finish their nonsense. There is a smell of kerosene oil and onions in the air. A lantern, always on hand for just such an emergency, burns in a corner. "Have you had a bad time in the trenches this week, Monsieur Levrault?" says the epiciere to a big, stolid soldier who is a regular customer.

"No, quite passable, Madame Champaubert."

"And Monsieur Petticollot, how is he?"

"Very well, thank you, madame. His captain was killed by a rifle grenade last week."

"Oh, the poor man."

Crash goes a shell. Everybody wonders where it has fallen. In a few seconds the eclats rain down into the street.

"Dirty animals," says the voice of the old man in the darkest of all the corners.

Madame Champaubert begins the story of how a cousin of hers who keeps a grocery-shop at Mailly, near the frontier, was cheated by a Boche tinware salesman. The cellar listens sympathetically. The boy says nothing, but keeps his eyes fixed on the soldiers. In about twenty minutes the bombardment ends, and the bolder ones go out to ascertain the damage. The soldier's purchases are lying on the counter. These he stuffs into his musette, the cloth wallet beloved of the poilu, and departs. The colonel's cook comes in; he has got hold of a good ham and wants to deck it out with herbs and capers. Has madame any capers? While she is getting them, the colonel's cook retails the cream of all the regimental gossip.

These people of Lorraine who have stayed behind, "Lorrains," the French term them, are thoroughly French, though there is some German blood in their veins. This Teuton addition is of very ancient date, being due to the constant invasions which have swept up the valley of the Moselle. This intermingling of the races, however, continued right up to 1870, but since then the union of French and German stock has been rare. It was most frequent, perhaps, during the years between 1804 and 1850, when Napoleon's domination of the principalities and states along the Rhine led to a French social and commercial invasion of Rhenish Germany, an invasion which ended only with the growth of German nationalism. The middle classes in particular intermarried because they were more apt to be engaged in commerce. But since 1870, two barriers, one geographic --annexed Lorraine, and one intellectual--hatred, have kept the neighbors apart. The Lorrain of to-day, no matter what his ancestors were, is a thorough Frenchman. These Lorrains are between medium height and tall, strongly built, with light, tawny hair, good color, and a brownish complexion.

The poilus who come to the village en repos are from every part of France, and are of all ages between nineteen and forty-five. I remember seeing a boy aged only fourteen who had enlisted, and was a regular member of an artillery regiment. The average regiment includes men of every class and caste, for every Frenchman who can shoulder a gun is in the war. Thus the dusty little soldier who is standing by Poste A, may be So-and-So the sculptor, the next man to him is simple Jacques who has a little farm near Bourges, and the man beyond, Emile, the notary's clerk. It is this amazing fraternity that makes the French army the greatest army in the world. The officers of a regiment of the active forces (by l'armee active you are to understand the army actually in the garrisons and under arms from year to year) are army officers by profession; the officers of the reserve regiments are either retired officers of the regular army or men who have voluntarily followed the severe courses in the officers' training-school. Thus the colonel and three of the commandants of a certain regiment were ex-officers of the regular army, while all the other officers, captains, lieutenants, and so forth, were citizens who followed civilian pursuits. Captain X was a famous lawyer, Captain B a small merchant in a little known provincial town, Captain C a photographer. Any Frenchman who has the requisite education can become an officer if he is willing to devote more of his time, than is by law required, to military service. Thus the French army is the soul of democracy, and the officer understands, and is understood by, his men. The spirit of the French army is remarkably fraternal, and this fraternity is at once social and mystical. It has a social origin, for the poilus realize that the army rests on class justice and equal opportunity; it has a mystical strength, because war has taught the men that it is only the human being that counts, and that comradeship is better than insistence on the rights and virtues of pomps and prides. After having been face to face with death for two years, a man learns something about the true values of human life.

The men who tramp into the village at one and two o'clock in the morning are men who have for two weeks been under a strain that two years of experience has robbed of its tensity. But strain it is, nevertheless, as the occasional carrying of a maniac reveals. They know very well why they are fighting; even the most ignorant French laborer has some idea as to what the affair is all about. The Boches attacked France who was peacefully minding her own business; it was the duty of all Frenchmen to defend France, so everybody went to the war. And since the war has gone on for so long, it must be seen through to the very end. Not a single poilu wants peace or is ready for peace. And the French, unlike the English, have continually under their eyes the spectacle of their devastated land. Yet I heard no ferocious talk about the Germans, no tales of French cruelty toward German prisoners.

Nevertheless, a German prisoner who had been taken in the Bois-le-Pretre confessed to me a horror of the French breaking through into Germany. Looking round to see if any one was listening, he said in English, for he was an educated man--"Just remember the French Revolution. Just remember the French Revolution. God! what cruelties. You remember Carrier at Nantes, don't you, my dear sir? All the things we are said to have done in Belgium--" But here the troop of prisoners was hurried to one side, and I never saw the man again. An army will always have all kinds of people in it, the good, the bad, the degenerate, the depraved, the brutal; and these types will act according to their natures. But I can't imagine several regiments of French poilus doing in little German towns what the Germans did at Nomeny. The backbone of the French army, as he is the backbone of France, is the French peasant. In spite of De Maupassant's ugly tales of the Norman country people, and Zola's studies of the sordid, almost bestial, life of certain unhappy, peasant families, the French peasant (cultivateur) is a very fine fellow. He has three very good qualities, endurance, patience, and willingness to work. Apart from these characteristics, he is an excellent fellow by himself; not jovial, to be sure, but solid, self-respecting, and glad to make friends when there is a chance that the friendship will be a real one. He does not care very much for the working men of the towns, the ouvriers, with their fantastic theories of universal brotherhood and peace, and he hates the depute whom the working man elects as he hates a vine fungus. A needless timidity, some fear of showing himself off as a simpleton, has kept him from having his just influence in French politics; but the war is freeing him from these shackles, and when peace comes, he will make himself known: that is, if there are any peasants left to vote.

Another thing about the peasantry is that trench warfare does not weary them, the constant contact with the earth having nothing unusual in it. A friend of mine, the younger son of a great landed family of the province of Anjou, was captain of a company almost exclusively composed of peasants of his native region; he loved them as if they were his children, and they would follow him anywhere. The little company, almost to a man, was wiped out in the battles round Verdun. In a letter I received from this officer, a few days before his death, he related this anecdote. His company was waiting, in a new trench in a new region, for the Germans to attack. Suddenly the tension was relieved by a fierce little discussion carried on entirely in whispers. His soldiers appeared to be studying the earth of the trench. "What's the trouble about?" he asked. Came the answer, "They are quarreling as to whether the earth of this trench would best support cabbages or turnips."

It is rare to find a French workman (ouvrier) in the trenches. They have all been taken out and sent home to make shells.

The little group to which I was most attached, and for whose hospitality and friendly greeting I shall always be a debtor, consisted of Belin, a railroad clerk; Bonnefon, a student at the Ecole des Beaux-Arts; Magne, a village schoolmaster in the Dauphine; and Gretry, proprietor of a butcher's shop in the Latin Quarter of Paris. Belin and Magne had violins which they left in the care of a cafe-keeper in the village, and used to play on them just before dinner. The dinner was served in the house of the village woman who prepared the food of these four, for sous-officiers are entitled to eat by themselves if they can find any one kind enough to look after the cooking. If they can't, then they have to rely entirely on the substantial but hardly delicious cuisine of their regimental cuistot. However, at this village, Madame Brun, the widow of the local carpenter, had offered to take the popotte, as the French term an officer's mess. We ate in a room half parlor, half bedchamber, decorated exclusively with holy pictures. This was a good specimen menu--bread, vermicelli soup, apple fritters, potato salad, boiled beef, red wine, and coffee. Of this dinner, the Government furnished the potatoes, the bread, the meat, the coffee, the wine, and the condiments; private purses paid for the fritters, the vermicelli, and the bits of onion in the salad. Standing round their barns the private soldiers were having a tasty stew of meat and potatoes cooked by the field kitchen, bread, and a cupful of boiled lentils (known in the army as "edible bedbugs"), all washed down with the army pinard, or red wine.

This village in which the troops were lodged revealed in an interesting way the course of French history. Across the river on a rise was a cross commemorating the victory of the Emperor Jo vin over the invading Germans in 371, and sunken in the bed of the Moselle were still seen lengths of Roman dikes. The heart of the village, however, was the corpse of a fourteenth-century castle which Richelieu had dismantled in 1630. Its destiny had been a curious one. Dismantled by Richelieu, sacked in the French Revolution, it had finally become a kind of gigantic mediaeval apartment house for the peasants of the region. The salle d'honneur was cut up into little rooms, the room of the seigneur became a haymow, and the cellars of the towers were used to store potatoes in. About twenty little chimneys rose over the old, dilapidated battlements. A haymow in this castle was the most picturesque thing I ever saw in a cantonment. It was the wreck of a lofty and noble fifteenth-century room, the ceiling, still a rich red brown, was supported on beautiful square beams, and a cross-barred window of the Renaissance, of which only the stonework remained, commanded a fine view over the river. The walls of the room were of stone, whitewashed years before, and the floor was an ordinary barn floor made of common planks and covered with a foot of new, clean hay. In the center of the southern wall was a Gothic fireplace, still black and ashy within. On the corners of this mantel hung clusters of canteens, guns were stacked by it, and a blue overcoat was rolled up at its base. An old man, the proprietor of the loft, followed us up, made signs that he was completely deaf, and traced in the dust on the floor the date, 1470.

The concerts were held in the "Salle de Fetes," a hall in which, during peace time, the village celebrates its little festivals. It was an ugly, bare shed with a sloping roof resting on iron girders painted clay white, but the poilus had beautified it with a home-made stage and rustic greenery. The proscenium arch, painted by Bonnefon, was pearl-gray in color and decorated with panels of gilt stripes; and a shield showing the lictor's rods, a red liberty cap and the letters "R. F." served as a headpiece. The scenery, also the work of Bonnefon, represented a Versailles kind of garden full of statues and very watery fountains. There was no curtain. Just below the stage a semicircle of chairs had been arranged for the officers of the regiment, and behind these were wooden benches and a large space for standing room. By the time the concert was supposed to begin, every bench was filled, and standing room was at a premium. Suddenly there were cries of "Le Colonel," and everybody stood up as the fine-looking old colonel and his staff took their places. The orchestra, composed of a pianist, a few violinists, and a flute-player, began to play the "Marseillaise." When the music was over, and everybody decently quiet, the concert began.

"Le Camarade Tollot, of the Theatre des Varietes de Paris will recite 'Le Dernier Drapeau,'" shouted the announcer. Le Camarade Tollot walked on the stage and bowed, a big, important young man with a lion's mane of dark hair. Then, striking an attitude, he recited in the best French, ranting style, a rhymed tale of a battle in which many regiments charged together, flags flying. One by one the flags fell to the ground as the bearers were cut down by the withering fire of the enemy; all save one who struggled on. It was a fine, old-fashioned, dramatic "will-he-get-there-yes-he-will-he-falls" sort of thing. "Il tombe," said le Camarade Tollot, in what used to be called the "oratorical orotund"--"il tombe." There was a full pause. He was wounded. He rose staggering to his feet. All the other flags were down. He advanced--the last flag (le dernier drapeau) reached the enemy--and died just as his comrades, heartened by his courage, had rallied and were charging to victory. A tremendous storm of applause greeted the speaker, who favored us with the recital of a short, sentimental poem as an encore.

The next number was thus announced: "Le Camarade Millet will sound, first, all the French bugle-calls and then the Boche ones." Le Camarade Millet, a big man with a fine horseshoe beard, stood at the edge of the stage, said, "la Charge francais" and blew it on the bugle; then "la Charge boche," and blew that. "La Retraite francais--La Retraite boche," etc. Another salvo of applause was given to le Camarade Millet.

"Le Camarade Roland."

Le Camarade Roland was about twenty-one or two years old, but his eyes were old and wise, and he had evidently seen life. He was dark-haired and a little below medium height. The red scar of a wound appeared just below his left ear. After marking time with his feet, he began a kind of patter song about having a telephone, every verse of which ended, "Oh, la la, j'ai le telephone chez moi" (I've a telephone in my house). "I know who is unfaithful now--who have horns upon their brow," the singer told of surprising secrets and unsuspected affaires de coeur. The silly, music-hall song may seem banal now, but it amused us hugely then. "Le Camarade Duclos."

"Oh, if you could have seen your son, My mother, my mother, Oh, if you could have seen your son, With the regiment"--sang Camarade Duclos, another old-eyed youngster. There was amiable adventure with an amiable "blonde" (oh, if you could have seen your son); another with a "jolie brune" (oh, ma mere, ma mere); and still another lecon d'amour. The refrain had a catchy lilt to it, and the poilus began humming it.

"Le Camarade Salvatore."

The newcomer was a big, obese Corsican mountaineer, with a pleasant, round face and brown eyes. He advanced quietly to the side of the stage holding a ten-sou tin flute in his hand, and when he began to play, for an instant I forgot all about the Bois-le-Pretre, the trenches, and everything else. The man was a born musician. I never heard anything more tender and sweet than the little melody he played. The poilus listened in profound silence, and when he had finished, a kind of sigh exhaled from the hearts of the audience.

There followed another singer, a violinist, and a clown whose song of a soldier on furlough finished with these appreciated couplets:--

"The Government says it is the thing To have a baby every spring; So when your son Is twenty-one, He'll come to the trenches and take papa's place. So do your duty by the race."

In the uproar of cheers of "That's right," and so on, the concert ended.

The day after the concert was Sunday, and at about ten o'clock that morning a young soldier with a fluffy, yellow chin beard came down the muddy street shouting, "le Mouchoir, le Mouchoir." About two or three hundred paper sheets were clutched tightly in his left hand, and he was selling them for a sou apiece. Little groups of poilus gathered round the soldier newsboy; I saw some of them laughing as they went away. The paper was the trench paper of the Bois-le-Pretre, named the "Mouchoir" (the handkerchief) from a famous position thus called in the Bois. The jokes in it were like the jokes in a local minstrel show, puns on local names, jests about the Boches, and good-humored satire. The spirit of the "Mouchoir" was whole-heartedly amateur. Thus the issue which followed a heavy snowfall contained this genuine wish:--

"Oh, snow, Please go, Leave the trench Of the French; Cross the band Of No Man's Land To where the Boche lies. Freeze him, Squeeze him, Soak him, Choke him, Cover him, Smother him, Till the beggar dies."

This is far from an exact translation, but the idea and the spirit have been faithfully preserved. The "Mouchoir" was always a bit more squeamish than the average, rollicking trench journal, for it was issued by a group of medical service men who were almost all priests. Indeed, there were some issues that combined satire, puns, and piety in a terrifying manner. Its editors printed it in the cellar of the church, using a simple sheet of gelatine for their press.

I wandered in to see the church. The usual number of civilians were to be seen, and a generous sprinkling of soldiers. Through the open door of the edifice the sounds of a mine-throwing competition at the Bois occasionally drifted. The abbe, a big, dark man of thirty-four or five, with a deep, resonant voice and positive gestures, had come to the sermon.

"Brethren," said he, "in place of a sermon this morning, I shall read the annual exposition of our Christian faith" (exposition de la foi chretienne). He began reading from a little book a historical account of the creation and the temptation, and so concise was the language and so certain his voice that I had the sensation of listening to a series of events that had actually taken place. He might have been reading the communique. "Le premier homme was called Adam, and la premiere femme, Eve. Certain angels began a revolt against God; they are called the bad angels or the demons." (Certains anges se sont mis en revolte contre Dieu; il sont appelles les mauvais anges ou les demons.) "And from this original sin arrives all the troubles, Death to which the human race is subjected." Such was the discourse I heard in the church by the trenches to the accompaniment of the distant chanting of The Wood.

Going by again late in the afternoon, I saw the end of an officer's funeral. The body, in a wooden box covered with the tricolor, was being carried out between two files of muddy soldiers, who stood at attention, bayonets fixed. A peasant's cart, a tumbril, was waiting to take the body to the cemetery; the driver was having a hard time con-trolling a foolish and restive horse. The colonel, a fine-looking man in the sixties, came last from the church, and stood on the steps surrounded by his officers. The dusk was falling.

"Officiers, sous-officiers, soldats.

"Lieutenant de Blanchet, whose death we deplore, was a gallant officer, a true comrade, and a loyal Frenchman. In order that France might live, he was willing to close his eyes on her forever."

The officer advanced to the tumbril and holding his hand high said:--

"Farewell--de Blanchet, we say unto thee the eternal adieu."

The door of the church was wide open. The sacristan put out the candles, and the smoke from them rose like incense into the air. The tumbril rattled away in the dusk. My mind returned again to the phrases of the sermon,--original sin, death, life, of a sudden, seemed strangely grotesque.

It would be hard to find any one more courteous and kind than the French officer. A good deal of the success of the American Ambulance Field Sections in France is due to the hospitality and bon acceuil of the French, and to the work of the French officers attached to the Sections. In Lieutenant Kuhlman, who commanded at Pont-a-Mousson, every American had a good friend and tactful, hard-working officer; in Lieutenant Maas, who commanded at Verdun, the qualities of administrative ability and perfect courtesy were most happily joined.

The principal characteristic of the French soldier is his reasonableness.

Chapter IX
Preparing The Defense Of Verdun

Every three months, if the military situation will allow of it and every other man in his group has likewise been away, the French soldier gets a six days' furlough. The slips of paper which are then given out are called feuilles de permission, and the lucky soldier is called a permissionnaire. When the combats that gave the Bois-le-Pretre its sinister nickname began to peter out, the poilus who had done the fighting were accorded these little vacations, and almost every afternoon the straggling groups of joyous permissionnaires were seen on the road between the trenches and the station. The expression on the faces was never that of having been rescued from a living hell; it expressed joy and prospect of a good time rather than deliverance.

When I got my permission, a comrade took me to the station at a certain railhead where a special train started for Paris, and by paying extra I was allowed to travel second class. I shall not dwell on the journey because I did not meet a single human being worth recording during the trip. At eight at night I arrived in Paris. So varied had been my experiences at the front that had I stepped out into a dark and deserted city I should not have been surprised. The poilu, when he sees the city lights again, almost feels like saying, "Why, it is still here!" Many of them look frankly at the women, not in the spirit of gallant adventure, but out of pure curiosity. In spite of the French reputation for roguish licentiousness, the sex question never seems to intrude very much along the battle-line, perhaps because there is so little to suggest it. Certainly conversation at the front ignores sex altogether, and speech there is remarkably decent and clean. Of course, when music-hall songs are sung at the concerts, the other sex is sometimes more than casually mentioned. It is the comic papers which are responsible for the myth that the period of furlough is spent in a Roman orgy; this is, of course, true of some few, but for the great majority the reverse rules, and une permission is spent in a typically French way, paying formal calls to the oldest friends of the family, being with the family as much as possible, and attending to such homely affairs as the purchase of socks and underclothes. In the evening brave Jacques or Georges or Francois is visited by all his old cronies, who gather round the hero and ask him questions, and he is solemnly kissed by all his relatives. One evening is sure to be consecrated to a grand family reunion at a restaurant.

I determined to observe, during my permission, the new France which has come into being since the outbreak of the war, and the attitude of the French toward their allies. I knew the old France pretty well. Putting any ridiculous ideas of French decadence aside, the France of the last ten years did not have the international standing of an older France. The Delcasse incident had revealed a France evidently untaught by the lesson of 1870, and if the Moroccan question ended in a French victory, it was frankly won by getting behind the petticoats of England. The nation was unprepared for war, torn by political strife, and in a position to be ruthlessly trampled on by the Germans. The France of 1900-13 is not a very pleasant France to remember.

For one thing, the bitter strife aroused by the breaking of the Concordat and the seizure of the property of the Church was slowly crystallizing into an icy hatred, the worst in the world, the hatred of a man who has been robbed. The Church Separation Law may have been right in theory, and with the liberal tendencies of the reformers one may have every sympathy, but the fact remains that the sale and dispersion of the ecclesiastical property passed in a storm of corruption and graft. Properties worth many thousands of dollars were juggled among political henchmen, sold for a song, and sold again at a great profit. Even as the Southerners complain of the Reconstruction rather than of the Civil War, so do the French Catholics complain, not of the law, but of its aftermath. The Socialist- Labor Party exultant, the Catholic Party wronged and revengeful, and all the other thousand parties of the French Government at one another's throats, there seemed little hope for the real France. The tragedy of the thing lay in the fact that this disunion and strife was caused by the excess of a good quality; in other words, that the remarkable ability of every Frenchman to think for himself was destroying the national unity.

Meanwhile, what was the state of the army and navy?

The Minister of War of the radicals who had triumphed was General Andre, a narrow, bigoted doctrinaire. The force behind the evil work of this man can be hardly realized by those who are unfamiliar with the passion with which the French invest the idea. There are times when the French, the most brilliant people in the world as a nation, seem to lack mental brakes--when the idea so obsesses them, that they become fanatics,--not the emotional, English type of fanatic, but a cold, hard-headed, intellectual Latin type. The radical Frenchman says, "Are the Gospels true?" "Presumably no, according to modern science and historical research." "Then away with everything founded on the Gospels," he replies; and begins a cold-blooded, highly intellectual campaign of destruction. Thus it is that the average French church or public building of any antiquity, whether it be in Paris or in an obscure village, has been so often mutilated that it is only a shadow of itself. France is strewn with wrecks of buildings embodying disputed ideas. And worst of all, these buildings were rarely sacked by a mob; the revolutionary commune, in many cases, paying laborers to smash windows and destroy sculpture at so much a day.

Andre believed it his mission to extirpate all conservatism, whether Catholic or not, from the army. In a few short months, by a campaign of delation and espionage, he had completely disorganized the army, the only really national institution left in France. Officers of standing, suspected of any reactionary political tendency, were discharged by the thousand; and officers against whom no charge could be brought were refused ammunition, even though they were stationed at a ticklish point on the frontier. At the same time a like disorganization was taking place in the navy, the evil genius of the Marine being the Minister Camille Pelletan.

Those who saw, in 1912, the ceremonies attendant on the deposition of the bones of Jean Jacques Rousseau in the Pantheon were sick at heart. Never had the Government of France sunk so low. The Royalists shouted, the extreme radicals hooted, and when the carriage of Fallieres passed, it was seen that humorists had somehow succeeded in writing jocose inscriptions on the presidential carriage. The head of the French nation, a short, pudgy man, the incarnation of pontifying mediocrity, went by with an expression on his face like that of a terrified, elderly, pink rabbit. The bescrawled carriage and its humiliated occupant passed by to an accompaniment of jeering. Everybody--parties and populace--was jeering. The scene was disgusting.

The election of Poincare, a man of genuine distinction, was a sign of better times. Millerand became Minister of War, and began the reorganization of the army, thus making possible the victory of the Marne. But a petty intrigue led by a group of radicals caused the resignation of this minister at a time when the First Balkan War threatened to engulf Europe. The maneuver was inexcusable. Messimy, an attache of the group who had led the attack, took Millerand's place. When the war broke out, Messimy was invited to make himself scarce, and Millerand returned to his post. Thanks to him, the army was as ready as an army in a democratic country can be.

The France of 1915-16 is a new France. The nation has learned that if it is to live it must cease tearing itself to pieces, and all parties are united in a "Holy Union" (l'Union Sacree). Truce in the face of a common danger or a real union? Will it last? Alarmists whisper that when the war is over, the army will settle its score with the politicians. Others predict a great victory for the radicals, because the industrial classes are safe at home making shells while the conservative peasants are being killed off in the trenches. Everybody in France is saying, "What will happen when the army comes home?" There is to-day only one man in France completely trusted by all classes--General Joffre, and if by any chance there should be political troubles after the war, the army and the nation will look to him.

The French fully realize what the English alliance has meant to them, and are grateful for Engish aid. As the titanic character of England's mighty effort becomes clearer, the sympathy with England will increase. Of course one cannot expect the French to understand the state of mind which insists upon a volunteer system in the face of the deadliest and most terrible foe. The attitude of the English to sport has rather perplexed them, and they did not like the action of some English officers in bringing a pack of hounds to the Flanders front. It was thought that officers should be soldiers first and sportsmen afterward, and the knowledge that dilettante English officers were riding to hounds while the English nation was resisting conscription and Jean, Jacques, and Pierre were doing the fighting and dying in the trenches, provoked a secret and bitter disdain.

But since the British have got into the war as a nation, this secret disdain has been forgotten, and the poilu has taken "le Tommie" to his heart.

I heard only the friendliest criticism of the Russians.

It is a rather delicate task to say what the French think of the Americans, for the real truth is that they think of us but rarely. Our quarrel with Germany over the submarines interested them somewhat, but this interest rapidly died away when it became evident that we were not going to do anything about it. They see our flag over countless charity depots, hospitals, and benevolent institutions, and are grateful. The poilu would be glad to see us in the fray simply because of the aid we should bring, but he is reasonable enough to know that the United States can keep out of the melee without losing any moral prestige. The only hostile criticism of America that I heard came from doctrinaires who saw the war as a conflict between autocracy and democracy, and if you grant that this point of view is the right one, these thinkers have a right to despise us. But the Frenchman knows that the Allies represent something more than "virtue-on-a-rampage."

In Lyons I saw a sight at once ludicrous and pathetic. Two little dragoons of the class of 1917, stripling boys of eighteen or nineteen at the most, walked across the public square; their uniforms were too large for them, the skirts of their great blue mantles barely hung above the dust of the street, and their enormous warlike helmets and flowing horse-tails were ill-suited to their boyish heads. As I looked at them, I thought of the blue bundles I had seen drying upon the barbed wire, and felt sick at the brutality of the whole awful business. The sun was shining over the bluish mists of Lyons, and the bell of old Saint-Jean was ringing. Two Zouaves, stone blind, went by guided by a little, fat infirmier. At the frontier, the General Staff was preparing the defense of Verdun.

One great nation, for the sake of a city valueless from a military point of view, was preparing to kill several hundred thousand of its citizens, and another great nation, anxious to retain the city, was preparing calmly for a parallel hecatomb. There is something awful and dreadful about the orderliness of a great offensive, for while one's imagination is grasped by the grandeur and the organization of the thing, all one's faculties of intellect are revolted by the stark brutality of death en masse.

Early in February we were called to Bar-le-Duc, a pleasant old city some distance behind Verdun. Several hundred thousand men were soon going to be killed and wounded, and the city was in a feverish haste of preparation. So many thousand cans of ether, so many thousand pounds of lint, so many million shells, so many ambulances, so many hundred thousand litres of gasoline. Nobody knew when the Germans were going to strike.

During the winter great activity in the German trenches near Verdun had led the French to expect an attack, but it was not till the end of January that aeroplane reconnoitering made certain the imminence of an offensive. As a first step in countering it, the French authorities prepared in the villages surrounding Bar-le-Duc a number of depots for troops, army supplies, and ammunition. Of this organization, Bar-le-Duc was the key. The preparations for the counter-attack were there centralized. Day after day convoys of motor-lorries carrying troops ground into town and disappeared to the eastward; big mortars mounted on trucks came rattling over the pavements to go no one knew where; and khaki-clad troops, troupes d'attaque, tanned Marocains and chunky, bull-necked Zouaves, crossed the bridge over the Ornain and marched away. At the turn in the road a new transparency had been erected, with VERDUN printed on it in huge letters. Now and then a soldier, catching sight of it, would nudge his comrade.

On the 18th we were told to be in readiness to go at any minute and permissions to leave the barrack yard were recalled.

The attack began with an air raid on Bar-le-Duc. I was working on my engine in the sunlit barrack yard when I heard a muffled Pom! somewhere to the right. Two French drivers who were putting a tire on their car jumped up with a "Qu'est-ce que c'est que ca?" We stood together looking round. Beyond a wall on the other side of the river great volumes of brownish smoke were rolling up, and high in the air, brown and silvery, like great locusts, were two German aeroplanes.

"Nom d'un chien, il y'en a plusieurs," said one of the Frenchmen, pointing out four, five, seven, nine aeroplanes. One seemed to hang immobile over the barrack yard. I fancy we all had visions of what would happen if a bomb hit the near-by gasoline reserve. Men ran across the yard to the shelter of the dormitories; some, caught as we were in the open, preferred to take a chance on dropping flat under a car. A whistling scream, a kind of shrill, increasing shriek, sounded in the air and ended in a crash. Smoke rolled up heavily in another direction. Another whistle, another crash, another and another and another. The last building struck shot up great tongues of flame. "C'est la gare," said somebody. Across the yard a comrade's arm beckoned me, "Come on, we've got to help put out the fires!"

The streets were quite deserted; horses and wagons abandoned to their fate were, however, quietly holding their places. Faces, emotionally divided between fear and strong interest, peered at us as we ran by, disappearing at the first whistle of a bomb, for all the world like hermit-crabs into their shells. A whistle sent us both scurrying into a passageway; the shell fell with a wicked hiss, and, scattering the paving-stones to the four winds, blew a shallow crater in the roadway. A big cart horse, hit in the neck and forelegs by fragments of the shell, screamed hideously. Right at the bridge, the sentry, an old territorial, was watching the whole scene from his flimsy box with every appearance of unconcern.

Not the station itself, but a kind of baggage-shed was on fire. A hose fed by an old-fashioned seesaw pump was being played on the flames. Officials of the railroad company ran to and fro shouting unintelligible orders. For five minutes more the German aeroplanes hovered overhead, then slowly melted away into the sky to the south-east. The raid had lasted, I imagine, just about twenty minutes.

That night, fearing another raid, all lights were extinguished in the town and at the barracks. Before rolling up in my blankets, I went out into the yard to get a few breaths of fresh air. Through the night air, rising and falling with the wind, I heard in one of the random silences of the night a low, distant drumming of artillery.

Chapter X
The Great Days of Verdun

The Verdun I saw in April, 1913, was an out-of-the-way provincial city of little importance outside of its situation as the nucleus of a great fortress. There were two cities--an old one, la ville des eveques, on a kind of acropolis rising from the left bank of the Meuse, and a newer one built on the meadows of the river. Round the acropolis Vauban had built a citadel whose steep, green-black walls struck root in the mean streets and narrow lanes on the slopes. Sunless by-ways, ill-paved and sour with the odor of surface drainage, led to it. Always picturesque, the old town now and then took on a real beauty. There were fine, shield-bearing doorways of the Renaissance to be seen, Gothic windows in greasy walls, and here and there at a street corner a huddle of half-timbered houses in a high contrast of invading sunlight and retreating shade. From the cathedral parapet, there was a view of the distant forts, and a horizontal sweep of the unharvested, buff-brown moorlands.

"Un peu morte," say the French who knew Verdun before the war. The new town was without distinction. It was out of date. It had none of the glories that the province copies from Paris, no boulevards, no grandes aerteres. Such life as there was, was military. Rue Mazel was bright with the gold braid and scarlet of the fournisseurs militaires, and in the late afternoon chic young officers enlivened the provincial dinginess with a brave show of handsome uniforms. All day long squads of soldiers went flick! flack! up and down the street and bugle-calls sounded piercingly from the citadel. The soldiery submerged the civil population.

With no industries of any importance, and becoming less and less of an economic center as the depopulation of the Woevre continued, Verdun lived for its garrison. A fortress since Roman days, the city could not escape its historic destiny. Remembering the citadel, the buttressed cathedral, the soldiery, and the military tradition, the visitor felt himself to be in a soldier's country strong with the memory of many wars.

The next day, at noon, we were ordered to go to M------, and at 12.15 we were in convoy formation in the road by the barracks wall. The great route nationale from Bar-le-Duc to Verdun runs through a rolling, buff-brown moorland, poor in villages and arid and desolate in aspect. Now it sinks through moorland valleys, now it cuts bowl-shaped depressions in which the spring rains have bred green quagmires, and now, rising, leaps the crest of a hill commanding a landscape of ocean-like immensity.

Gray segments of the road disappear ahead behind fuzzy monticules; a cloud of wood-smoke hangs low over some invisible village in a fold of the moor, and patches of woodland lie like mantles on the barren slopes. Great swathes of barbed wire, a quarter of a mile in width, advancing and retreating, rising and falling with the geographical nature of the defensive position, disappear on both sides to the horizon. And so thick is this wire spread, that after a certain distance the eye fails to distinguish the individual threads and sees only rows of stout black posts filled with a steely, purple mist.

We went though several villages, being greeted in every one with the inevitable error, Anglais! We dodged interminable motor-convoys carrying troops, the poilus sitting unconcernedly along the benches at the side, their rifles tight between their knees. At midnight we arrived at B------, four miles and a half west of Verdun. The night was clear and bitter cold; the ice-blue winter stars were westering. Refugees tramped past in the darkness. By the sputtering light of a match, I saw a woman go by with a cat in a canary cage; the animal moved uneasily, its eyes shone with fear. A middle-aged soldier went by accompanying an old woman and a young girl. Many pushed baby carriages ahead of them full of knick-knacks and packages.

The crossroad where the ambulances turned off was a maze of beams of light from the autos. There was shouting of orders which nobody could carry out. Wounded, able to walk, passed through the beams of the lamps, the red of their bloodstains, detached against the white of the bandages, presenting the sharpest of contrasts in the silvery glare. At the station, men who had died in the ambulances were dumped hurriedly in a plot of grass by the side of the roadway and covered with a blanket. Never was there seen such a bedlam! But on the main road the great convoys moved smoothly on as if held together by an invisible chain. A smouldering in the sky told of fires in Verdun.

From a high hill between B------and Verdun I got my first good look at the bombardment. From the edge of earth and sky, far across the moorlands, ray after ray of violet-white fire made a swift stab at the stars. Mingled with the rays, now seen here, now there, the reddish-violet semicircle of the great mortars flared for the briefest instant above the horizon. From the direction of this inferno came a loud roaring, a rumbling and roaring, increasing in volume--the sound of a great river tossing huge rocks through subterranean abysses. Every little while a great shell, falling in the city, would blow a great hole of white in the night, and so thundering was the crash of arrival that we almost expected to see the city sink into the earth.

Terrible in the desolation of the night, on fire, haunted by specters of wounded men who crept along the narrow lanes by the city walls, Verdun was once more undergoing the destinies of war. The shells were falling along rue Mazel and on the citadel. A group of old houses by the Meuse had burnt to rafters of flickering flame, and as I passed them, one collapsed into the flooded river in a cloud of hissing steam.

In order to escape shells, the wounded were taking the obscure by-ways of the town. Our wounded had started to walk to the ambulance station with the others, but, being weak and exhausted, had collapsed on the way. They were waiting for us at a little house just beyond the walls. Said one to the other, "As-tu-vu Maurice?" and the other answered without any emotion, "Il est mort."

The 24th was the most dreadful day. The wind and snow swept the heights of the desolate moor, seriously interfering with the running of the automobiles. Here and there, on a slope, a lorry was stuck in the slush, though the soldier passengers were out of it and doing their best to push it along. The cannonade was still so intense that, in intervals between the heavier snow-flurries, I could see the stabs of fire in the brownish sky. Wrapped in sheepskins and muffled to the ears in knitted scarves that might have come from New England, the territorials who had charge of the road were filling the ruts with crushed rock. Exhaustion had begun to tell on the horses; many lay dead and snowy in the frozen fields. A detachment of khaki-clad, red-fezzed colonial troops passed by, bent to the storm. The news was of the most depressing sort. The wounded could give you only the story of their part of the line, and you heard over and over again, "Nous avons recules." A detachment of cavalry was at hand; their casques and dark-blue mantles gave them a crusading air. And through the increasing cold and darkness of late afternoon, troops, cannons, horsemen, and motor-trucks vanished toward the edge of the moor where flashed with increasing brilliance the rays of the artillery.

I saw some German prisoners for the first time at T---, below Verdun. They had been marched down from the firing-line. Young men in the twenties for the most part, they seemed even more war-worn than the French. The hideous, helot-like uniform of the German private hung loosely on their shoulders, and the color of their skin was unhealthy and greenish. They were far from appearing starved; I noticed two or three who looked particularly sound and hearty. Nevertheless, they were by no means as sound-looking as the ruddier French.

The poilus crowded round to see them, staring into their faces without the least malevolence. At last--at last--voila enfin des Boches! A little to the side stood a strange pair, two big men wearing an odd kind of grayish protector and apron over their bodies. Against a near-by wall stood a kind of flattish tank to which a long metallic hose was attached. The French soldiers eyed them with contempt and disgust. I caught the words, "Flame-throwers!"

I do not know what we should have done at Verdun without Lieutenant Roeder, our mechanical officer. All the boys behaved splendidly, but Lieutenant Roeder had the tremendously difficult task of keeping the Section going when the rolling-stock was none too good, and fearful weather and too constant usage had reduced some of the wagons to wrecks. It was all the finer of him because he was by profession a bacteriologist. Still very young, he had done distinguished work. Simply because there was no one else to attend to the mechanical department, he had volunteered for this most tiresome and disagreeable task. There is not a single driver in Section II who does not owe much to the friendly counsel, splendid courage, and keen mind of George Roeder.

A few miles below Verdun, on a narrow strip of meadowland between the river and the northern bluffs, stood an eighteenth-century chateau and the half-dozen houses of its dependents. The hurrying river had flooded the low fields and then retreated, turning the meadows and pasturages to bright green, puddly marshes, malodorous with swampy exhalations. Beyond the swirls and currents of the river and its vanishing islands of pale-green pebbles, rose the brown, deserted hills of the Hauts de Meuse. The top of one height had been pinched into the rectangle of a fortress; little forests ran along the sky-line of the heights, and a narrow road, slanting across a spur of the valley, climbed and disappeared.

The chateau itself was a huge, three-story box of gray-white stone with a slate roof, a little turret en poivriere at each corner, and a graceless classic doorway in the principal facade. A wide double gate, with a coronet in a tarnished gold medallion set in the iron arch-piece, gave entrance to this place through a kind of courtyard formed by the rear of the chateau and the walls of two low wings devoted to the stables and the servants' quarters. Within, a high clump of dark- green myrtle, ringed with muddy, rut-scarred turf, marked the theoretical limits of a driveway. Along the right-hand wall stood the rifles of the wounded, and in a corner, a great snarled pile of bayonets, belts, cartridge-boxes, gas-mask satchels, greasy tin boxes of anti-lice ointment, and dented helmets. A bright winter sunlight fell on walls dank from the river mists, and heightened the austerity of the landscape. Beyond a bend in the river lay the smoke of the battle of Douaumont; shells broke, pin-points of light, in the upper fringes of the haze.

The chateau had been a hospital since the beginning of the war. A heavy smell of ether and iodoform lay about it, mixed with the smell of the war. This effluvia of an army, mixed with the sharper reek of anaesthetics, was the atmosphere of the hospital. The great rush of wounded had begun. Every few minutes the ambulances slopped down a miry byway, and turned in the gates; tired, putty-faced hospital attendants took out the stretchers and the nouveaux clients; mussy bundles of blue rags and bloody blankets turned into human beings; an overworked, nervous medecin chef shouted contradictory orders at the brancardiers, and passed into real crises of hysterical rage.

"Avancez!" he would scream at the bewildered chauffeurs of the ambulances; and an instant later, "Reculez! Reculez!"

The wounded in the stretchers, strewn along the edges of the driveway, raised patient, tired eyes at his snarling.

Another doctor, a little bearded man wearing a white apron and the red velvet kepi of an army physician, questioned each batch of new arrivals. Deep lines of fatigue had traced themselves under his kindly eyes; his thin face had a dreadful color. Some of the wounded had turned their eyes from the sun; others, too weak to move, lay stonily blinking. Almost expressionless, silent, they resigned themselves to the attendants as if these men were the deaf ministers of some inexorable power.

The surgeon went from stretcher to stretcher looking at the diagnosis cards attached at the poste de secours, stopping occasionally to ask the fatal question, "As-tu crache du sang?" (Have you spit blood?) A thin oldish man with a face full of hollows like that of an old horse, answered "Oui," faintly. Close by, an artilleryman, whose cannon had burst, looked with calm brown eyes out of a cooked and bluish face. Another, with a soldier's tunic thrown capewise over his naked torso, trembled in his thin blanket, and from the edges of a cotton and lint-pad dressing hastily stuffed upon a shoulder wound, an occasional drop of blood slid down his lean chest.

A little to one side, the cooks of the hospital, in their greasy aprons, watched the performance with a certain calm interest. In a few minutes the wounded were sorted and sent to the various wards. I was ordered to take three men who had been successfully operated on to the barracks for convalescents several miles away.

A highway and an unused railroad, both under heavy fire from German guns on the Hauts de Meuse, passed behind the chateau and along the foot of the bluffs. There were a hundred shell holes in the marshes between the road and the river, black-lipped craters in the sedgy green; there were ugly punches in the brown earth of the bluffs, and deep scoops in the surface of the road. The telephone wires, cut by shell fragments, fell in stiff, draping lines to the ground. Every once in a while a shell would fall into the river, causing a silvery gray geyser to hang for an instant above the green eddies of the Meuse. A certain village along this highway was the focal point of the firing. Many of the houses had been blown to pieces, and fragments of red tile, bits of shiny glass, and lumps of masonry were strewn all over the deserted street.

As I hurried along, two shells came over, one sliding into the river with a Hip!

and the other landing in a house about two hundred yards away. A vast cloud of grayish-black smoke befogged the cottage, and a section of splintered timber came buzzing through the air and fell into a puddle. From the house next to the one struck, a black cat came slinking, paused for an indecisive second in the middle of the street, and ran back again. Through the canvas partition of the ambulance, I heard the voices of my convalescents. "No more marmites!" I cried to them as I swung down a road out of shell reach. I little knew what was waiting for us beyond the next village.

A regiment of Zouaves going up to the line was resting at the crossroad, and the regimental wagons, drawn up in waiting line, blocked the narrow road completely. At the angle between the two highways, under the four trees planted by pious custom of the Meuse, stood a cross of thick planks. From each arm of the cross, on wine-soaked straps, dangled, like a bunch of grapes, a cluster of dark-blue canteens; rifles were stacked round its base, and under the trees stood half a dozen clipped-headed, bull-necked Zouaves. A rather rough-looking adjutant, with a bullet head disfigured by a frightful scar at the corner of his mouth, rode up and down the line to see if all was well. Little groups were handing round a half loaf of army bread, and washing it down with gulps of wine.

"Hello, sport!" they cried at me; and the favorite "All right," and "Tommy!"

The air was heavy with the musty smell of street mud that never dries during winter time, mixed with the odor of the tired horses, who stood, scarcely moving, backed away from their harnesses against the mire-gripped wagons. Suddenly the order to go on again was given; the carters snapped their whips, the horses pulled, the noisy, lumbering, creaky line moved on, and the men fell in behind, in any order.

I started my car again and looked for an opening through the melee.

Beyond the cross, the road narrowed and flanked one of the southeastern forts of the city. A meadow, which sloped gently upward from the road to the abrupt hillside of the fortress, had been used as a place of encampment and had been trodden into a surface of thick cheesy mire. Here and there were the ashes of fires. There were hundreds of such places round the moorland villages between Verdun and Bar-le-Duc. The fort looked squarely down on Verdun, and over its grassy height came the drumming of the battle, and the frequent crash of big shells falling into the city.

In a corner lay the anatomical relics of some horses killed by an air-bomb the day before. And even as I noted them, I heard the muffled Pom! Pom! Pom! of anti-aircraft guns. My back was to the river and I could not see what was going on.

"What is it?" I said to a Zouave who was plodding along beside the ambulance.

"Des Boches--crossing the river."

The regiment plodded on as before. Now and then a soldier would stop and look up at the aeroplanes.

"He's coming!" I heard a voice exclaim.

Suddenly, the adjutant whom I had seen before came galloping down the line, shouting, "Arretez! Arretez! Pas de mouvement!"

A current of tension ran down the troop with as much reality as a current of water runs down hill. I wondered whether the Boche had seen us.

"Is he approaching?" I asked.

"Yes."

Ahead of me was a one-horse wagon, and ahead of that a wagon with two horses carrying the medical supplies. The driver of the latter, an oldish, thick-set, wine-faced fellow, got down an instant from his wagon, looked at the Boche, and resumed his seat. A few seconds later, there sounded the terrifying scream of an air-bomb, a roar, and I found myself in a bitter swirl of smoke. The shell had fallen right between the horses of the two-horse wagon, blowing the animals to pieces, splintering the wagon, and killing the driver. Something sailed swiftly over my head, and landed just behind the ambulance. It was a chunk of the skull of one of the horses. The horse attached to the wagon ahead of me went into a frenzy of fear and backed his wagon into my ambulance, smashing the right lamp. In the twinkling of an eye, the soldiers dispersed. Some ran into the fields. Others crouched in the wayside ditch. A cart upset. Another bomb dropped screaming in a field and burst; a cloud of smoke rolled away down the meadow.

When the excitement had subsided, it was found that a soldier had been wounded. The bodies of the horses were rolled over into the ditch, the wreck of the wagon was dragged to the miry field, and the regiment went on. In a very short time I got to the hospital and delivered my convalescents.

My way home ran through the town of S------, an ugly, overgrown village of the Verdunois, given up to the activities of the staff directing the battle. The head-quarters building was the hotel de ville, a large eighteenth-century edifice, in an acre of trampled mud a little distance from the street. Before the building flowed the great highway from Bar-le-Duc to Verdun; relays of motor lorries went by, and gendarmes, organized into a kind of traffic squad, stood every hundred feet or so. The atmosphere of S------at the height of the battle was one of calm organization; it would not have been hard to believe that the motor-lorries and unemotional men were at the service of some great master-work of engineering. There was something of the holiday in the attitude of the inhabitants of the place; they watched the motor show exactly as they might have watched a circus parade.

"Les voila," said somebody.

A little bemedaled group appeared on the steps of the hotel de ville. Dominating it was Joffre. Above middle height, silver-haired, elderly, he has a certain paternal look which his eye belies; Joffre's eye is the hard eye of a commander-in-chief, the military eye, the eye of an Old Testament father if you will. De Castelnau was speaking, making no gestures--an old man with an ashen skin, deep-set eye and great hooked nose, a long cape concealed the thick, age-settled body. Poincare stood listening, with a look at once worried and brave, the ghost of a sad smile lingering on a sensitive mouth. Last of all came Petain, the protege of De Castelnau, who commanded at Verdun--a tall, square-built man, not un-English in his appearance, with grizzled hair and the sober face of a thinker. But his mouth and jaw are those of a man of action, and the look in his gray eyes is always changing. Now it is speculative and analytic, now steely and cold.

In the shelter of a doorway stood a group of territorials, getting their first real news of the battle from a Paris newspaper. I heard "Nous avons recule--huit kilo-metres--le general Petain--" A motor-lorry drowned out the rest.

That night we were given orders to be ready to evacuate the chateau in case the Boches advanced. The drivers slept in the ambulances, rising at intervals through the night to warm their engines. The buzz of the motors sounded through the tall pines of the chateau park, drowning out the rumbling of the bombardment and the monotonous roaring of the flood. Now and then a trench light, rising like a spectral star over the lines on the Hauts de Meuse, would shine reflected in the river.

At intervals attendants carried down the swampy paths to the chapel the bodies of soldiers who had died during the night. The cannon flashing was terrific. Just before dawn, half a dozen batteries of "seventy-fives" came in a swift trot down the shelled road; the men leaned over on their steaming horses, the harnesses rattled and jingled, and the cavalcade swept on, outlined a splendid instant against the mortar flashes and the streaks of day.

On my morning trip a soldier with bandaged arm was put beside me on the front seat. He was about forty years old; a wiry black beard gave a certain fullness to his thin face, and his hands were pudgy and short of finger. When he removed his helmet, I saw that he was bald. A bad cold caused him to speak in a curious whispering tone, giving to everything he said the character of a grotesque confidence.

"What do you do en civil?" he asked.

I told him.

"I am a pastry cook," he went on; "my specialty is Saint-Denis apple tarts."

A marmite intended for the road landed in the river as he spoke.

"Have you ever had one? They are very good when made with fresh cream." He sighed.

"How did you get wounded?" said I.

"Eclat d'obus," he replied, as if that were the whole story. After a pause he added, "Douaumont--yesterday."

I thought of the shells I had seen bursting over the fort.

"Do you put salt in chocolate?" he asked professionally.

"Not as a rule," I replied.

"It improves it," he pursued, as if he were revealing a confidential dogma. "The Boche bread is bad, very bad, much worse than a year ago. Full of crumbles and lumps. Degoutant!"

The ambulance rolled up to the evacuation station, and my pastry cook alighted.

"When the war is over, come to my shop," he whispered benevolently, "and you shall have some tartes aux pommes a la mode de Saint-Denis with my wife and me."

"With fresh cream?" I asked.

"Of course," he replied seriously.

I accepted gratefully, and the good old soul gave me his address.

In the afternoon a sergeant rode with me. He was somewhere between twenty-eight and thirty, thick-set of body, with black hair and the tanned and ruddy complexion of outdoor folk. The high collar of a dark-blue sweater rose over his great coat and circled a muscular throat; his gray socks were pulled country-wise outside of the legs of his blue trousers. He had an honest, pleasant face; there was a certain simple, wholesome quality about the man. In the piping times of peace, he was a cultivateur in the Valois, working his own little farm; he was married and had two little boys. At Douaumont, a fragment of a shell had torn open his left hand.

"The Boches are not going to get through up there?"

"Not now. As long as we hold the heights, Verdun is safe." His simple French, innocent of argot, had a good country twang. "But oh, the people killed! Comme il y a des gens tues!" He pronounced the final s of the word gens in the manner of the Valois.

"Ca s'accroche aux arbres," he continued.

The vagueness of the ca had a dreadful quality in it that made you see trees and mangled bodies. "We had to hold the crest of Douaumont under a terrible fire, and clear the craters on the slope when the Germans tried to fortify them. Our 'seventy-fives' dropped shells into the big craters as I would drop stones into a pond. Pauvres gens!"

The phrase had an earth-wide sympathy in it, a feeling that the translation "poor folks" does not render. He had taken part in a strange incident. There had been a terrible corps-a-corps in one of the craters which had culminated in a victory for the French; but the lieutenant of his company had left a kinsman behind with the dead and wounded. Two nights later, the officer and the sergeant crawled down the dreadful slope to the crater where the combat had taken place, in the hope of finding the wounded man. They could hear faint cries and moans from the crater before they got to it. The light of a pocket flash-lamp showed them a mass of dead and wounded on the floor of the crater--"un tas de mourants et de cadavres," as he expressed it.

After a short search, they found the man for whom they were looking; he was still alive but unconscious. They were dragging him out when a German, hideously wounded, begged them to kill him.

"Moi, je n'ai plus jambes," he repeated in French; "pitie, tuez-moi."

He managed to make the lieutenant see that if he went away and left them, they would all die in the agonies of thirst and open wounds. A little flickering life still lingered in a few; there were vague rales in the darkness. A rafale of shells fell on the slope; the violet glares outlined the mouth of the crater.

"Ferme tes yeux" (shut your eyes), said the lieutenant to the German. The Frenchmen scrambled over the edge of the crater with their unconscious burden, and then, from a little distance, threw hand-grenades into the pit till all the moaning died away.

Two weeks later, when the back of the attack had been broken and the organization of the defense had developed into a trusted routine, I went again to Verdun. The snow was falling heavily, covering the piles of debris and sifting into the black skeletons of the burned houses. Untrodden in the narrow streets lay the white snow. Above the Meuse, above the ugly burned areas in the old town on the slope, rose the shell-spattered walls of the citadel and the cathedral towers of the still, tragic town. The drumming of the bombardment had died away. The river was again in flood. In a deserted wine-shop on a side street well protected from shells by a wall of sandbags was a post of territorials.

To the tragedy of Verdun, these men were the chorus; there was something Sophoclean in this group of older men alone in the silence and ruin of the beleaguered city. A stove filled with wood from the wrecked houses gave out a comfortable heat, and in an alley-way, under cover, stood a two-wheeled hose cart, and an old-fashioned seesaw fire pump. There were old clerks and bookkeepers among the soldier firemen--retired gendarmes who had volunteered, a country schoolmaster, and a shrewd peasant from the Lyonnais. Watch was kept from the heights of the citadel, and the outbreak of fire in any part of the city was telephoned to the shop. On that day only a few explosive shells had fallen.

"Do you want to see something odd, mon vieux?" said one of the pompiers to me; and he led me through a labyrinth of cellars to a cold, deserted house. The snow had blown through the shell-splintered window-panes. In the dining-room stood a table, the cloth was laid and the silver spread; but a green feathery fungus had grown in a dish of food and broken straws of dust floated on the wine in the glasses. The territorial took my arm, his eyes showing the pleasure of my responding curiosity, and whispered,--

"There were officers quartered here who were called very suddenly. I saw the servant of one of them yesterday; they have all been killed."

Outside there was not a flash from the batteries on the moor. The snow continued to fall, and darkness, coming on the swift wings of the storm, fell like a mantle over the desolation of the city.

The End

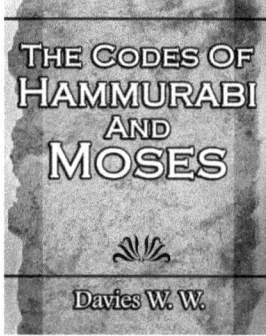

The Codes Of Hammurabi And Moses
W. W. Davies

QTY

The discovery of the Hammurabi Code is one of the greatest achievements of archaeology, and is of paramount interest, not only to the student of the Bible, but also to all those interested in ancient history...

Religion   **ISBN:** *1-59462-338-4*   **Pages:132**
MSRP $12.95

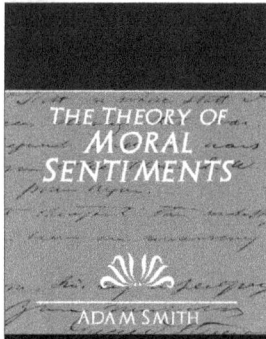

The Theory of Moral Sentiments
Adam Smith

QTY

This work from 1749. contains original theories of conscience amd moral judgment and it is the foundation for systemof morals.

Philosophy   **ISBN:** *1-59462-777-0*   **Pages:536**
MSRP $19.95

Jessica's First Prayer
Hesba Stretton

QTY

In a screened and secluded corner of one of the many railway-bridges which span the streets of London there could be seen a few years ago, from five o'clock every morning until half past eight, a tidily set-out coffee-stall, consisting of a trestle and board, upon which stood two large tin cans, with a small fire of charcoal burning under each so as to keep the coffee boiling during the early hours of the morning when the work-people were thronging into the city on their way to their daily toil...

Pages:84

Childrens   **ISBN:** *1-59462-373-2*   *MSRP $9.95*

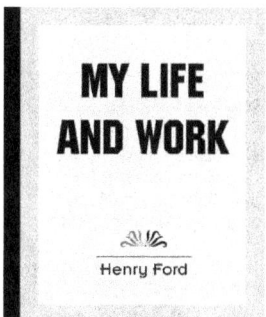

My Life and Work
Henry Ford

QTY

Henry Ford revolutionized the world with his implementation of mass production for the Model T automobile. Gain valuable business insight into his life and work with his own auto-biography... "We have only started on our development of our country we have not as yet, with all our talk of wonderful progress, done more than scratch the surface. The progress has been wonderful enough but..."

Pages:300

Biographies/   **ISBN:** *1-59462-198-5*   *MSRP $21.95* www.bookjungle.com *email: sales@bookjungle.com fax: 630-214-0564 mail: Book Jungle PO Box 2226 Champaign, IL 61825*

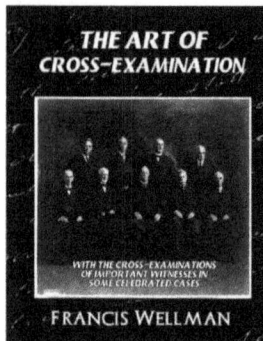

The Art of Cross-Examination
Francis Wellman

I presume it is the experience of every author, after his first book is published upon an important subject, to be almost overwhelmed with a wealth of ideas and illustrations which could readily have been included in his book, and which to his own mind, at least, seem to make a second edition inevitable. Such certainly was the case with me; and when the first edition had reached its sixth impression in five months, I rejoiced to learn that it seemed to my publishers that the book had met with a sufficiently favorable reception to justify a second and considerably enlarged edition. ..

Pages:412

Reference   ISBN: *1-59462-647-2*   *MSRP $19.95*

QTY

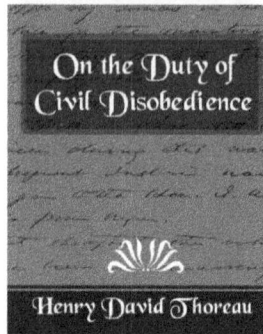

On the Duty of Civil Disobedience
Henry David Thoreau

Thoreau wrote his famous essay, On the Duty of Civil Disobedience, as a protest against an unjust but popular war and the immoral but popular institution of slave-owning. He did more than write—he declined to pay his taxes, and was hauled off to gaol in consequence. Who can say how much this refusal of his hastened the end of the war and of slavery ?

Law   ISBN: *1-59462-747-9*   **Pages:48**
MSRP $7.45

QTY

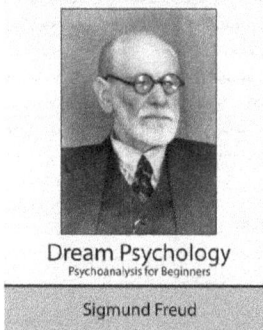

Dream Psychology Psychoanalysis for Beginners
Sigmund Freud

Sigmund Freud, born Sigismund Schlomo Freud (May 6, 1856 - September 23, 1939), was a Jewish-Austrian neurologist and psychiatrist who co-founded the psychoanalytic school of psychology. Freud is best known for his theories of the unconscious mind, especially involving the mechanism of repression; his redefinition of sexual desire as mobile and directed towards a wide variety of objects; and his therapeutic techniques, especially his understanding of transference in the therapeutic relationship and the presumed value of dreams as sources of insight into unconscious desires.

Pages:196

Psychology   ISBN: *1-59462-905-6*   *MSRP $15.45*

QTY

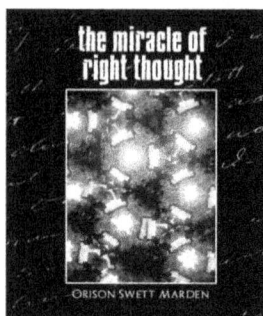

The Miracle of Right Thought
Orison Swett Marden

Believe with all of your heart that you will do what you were made to do. When the mind has once formed the habit of holding cheerful, happy, prosperous pictures, it will not be easy to form the opposite habit. It does not matter how improbable or how far away this realization may see, or how dark the prospects may be, if we visualize them as best we can, as vividly as possible, hold tenaciously to them and vigorously struggle to attain them, they will gradually become actualized, realized in the life. But a desire, a longing without endeavor, a yearning abandoned or held indifferently will vanish without realization.

Pages:360

Self Help   ISBN: *1-59462-644-8*   *MSRP $25.45*

QTY

The Rosicrucian Cosmo-Conception Mystic Christianity by *Max Heindel*   ISBN: *1-59462-188-8* **$38.95**
The Rosicrucian Cosmo-conception is not dogmatic, neither does it appeal to any other authority than the reason of the student. It is; not controversial, but is: sent forth in the, hope that it may help to clear...   New Age/Religion Pages 646

Abandonment To Divine Providence by *Jean-Pierre de Caussade*   ISBN: *1-59462-228-0* **$25.95**
"The Rev. Jean Pierre de Caussade was one of the most remarkable spiritual writers of the Society of Jesus in France in the 18th Century. His death took place at Toulouse in 1751. His works have gone through many editions and have been republished...   Inspirational/Religion Pages 400

Mental Chemistry by *Charles Haanel*   ISBN: *1-59462-192-6* **$23.95**
Mental Chemistry allows the change of material conditions by combining and appropriately utilizing the power of the mind. Much like applied chemistry creates something new and unique out of careful combinations of chemicals the mastery of mental chemistry...   New Age Pages 354

The Letters of Robert Browning and Elizabeth Barret Barrett 1845-1846 vol II   ISBN: *1-59462-193-4* **$35.95**
by *Robert Browning* and *Elizabeth Barrett*   Biographies Pages 596

Gleanings In Genesis (volume I) by *Arthur W. Pink*   ISBN: *1-59462-130-6* **$27.45**
Appropriately has Genesis been termed "the seed plot of the Bible" for in it we have, in germ form, almost all of the great doctrines which are afterwards fully developed in the books of Scripture which follow...   Religion/Inspirational Pages 420

The Master Key by *L. W. de Laurence*   ISBN: *1-59462-001-6* **$30.95**
In no branch of human knowledge has there been a more lively increase of the spirit of research during the past few years than in the study of Psychology, Concentration and Mental Discipline. The requests for authentic lessons in Thought Control, Mental Discipline and...   New Age/Business Pages 422

The Lesser Key Of Solomon Goetia by *L. W. de Laurence*   ISBN: *1-59462-092-X* **$9.95**
This translation of the first book of the "Lernegton" which is now for the first time made accessible to students of Talismanic Magic was done, after careful collation and edition, from numerous Ancient Manuscripts in Hebrew, Latin, and French...   New Age/Occult Pages 92

Rubaiyat Of Omar Khayyam by *Edward Fitzgerald*   ISBN:*1-59462-332-5* **$13.95**
Edward Fitzgerald, whom the world has already learned, in spite of his own efforts to remain within the shadow of anonymity, to look upon as one of the rarest poets of the century, was born at Bredfield, in Suffolk, on the 31st of March, 1809. He was the third son of John Purcell...   Music Pages 172

Ancient Law by *Henry Maine*   ISBN: *1-59462-128-4* **$29.95**
The chief object of the following pages is to indicate some of the earliest ideas of mankind, as they are reflected in Ancient Law, and to point out the relation of those ideas to modern thought.   Religion/History Pages 452

Far-Away Stories by *William J. Locke*   ISBN: *1-59462-129-2* **$19.45**
"Good wine needs no bush,' but a collection of mixed vintages does. And this book is just such a collection. Some of the stories I do not want to remain buried for ever in the museum files of dead magazine-numbers an author's not unpardonable vanity..."   Fiction Pages 272

Life of David Crockett by *David Crockett*   ISBN: *1-59462-250-7* **$27.45**
"Colonel David Crockett was one of the most remarkable men of the times in which he lived. Born in humble life, but gifted with a strong will, an indomitable courage, and unremitting perseverance...   Biographies/New Age Pages 424

Lip-Reading by *Edward Nitchie*   ISBN: *1-59462-206-X* **$25.95**
Edward B. Nitchie, founder of the New York School for the Hard of Hearing, now the Nitchie School of Lip-Reading, Inc, wrote "LIP-READING Principles and Practice". The development and perfecting of this meritorious work on lip-reading was an undertaking...   How-to Pages 400

A Handbook of Suggestive Therapeutics, Applied Hypnotism, Psychic Science   ISBN: *1-59462-214-0* **$24.95**
by *Henry Munro*   Health/New Age/Health/Self-help Pages 376

A Doll's House: and Two Other Plays by *Henrik Ibsen*   ISBN: *1-59462-112-8* **$19.95**
Henrik Ibsen created this classic when in revolutionary 1848 Rome. Introducing some striking concepts in playwriting for the realist genre, this play has been studied the world over.   Fiction/Classics/Plays 308

The Light of Asia by *sir Edwin Arnold*   ISBN: *1-59462-204-3* **$13.95**
In this poetic masterpiece, Edwin Arnold describes the life and teachings of Buddha. The man who was to become known as Buddha to the world was born as Prince Gautama of India but he rejected the worldly riches and abandoned the reigns of power when...   Religion/History/Biographies Pages 170

The Complete Works of Guy de Maupassant by *Guy de Maupassant*   ISBN: *1-59462-157-8* **$16.95**
"For days and days, nights and nights, I had dreamed of that first kiss which was to consecrate our engagement, and I knew not on what spot I should put my lips..."   Fiction/Classics Pages 240

The Art of Cross-Examination by *Francis L. Wellman*   ISBN: *1-59462-309-0* **$26.95**
Written by a renowned trial lawyer, Wellman imparts his experience and uses case studies to explain how to use psychology to extract desired information through questioning.   How-to/Science/Reference Pages 408

Answered or Unanswered? by *Louisa Vaughan*   ISBN: *1-59462-248-5* **$10.95**
Miracles of Faith in China   Religion Pages 112

The Edinburgh Lectures on Mental Science (1909) by *Thomas*   ISBN: *1-59462-008-3* **$11.95**
This book contains the substance of a course of lectures recently given by the writer in the Queen Street Hall, Edinburgh. Its purpose is to indicate the Natural Principles governing the relation between Mental Action and Material Conditions...   New Age/Psychology Pages 148

Ayesha by *H. Rider Haggard*   ISBN: *1-59462-301-5* **$24.95**
Verily and indeed it is the unexpected that happens! Probably if there was one person upon the earth from whom the Editor of this, and of a certain previous history, did not expect to hear again...   Classics Pages 380

Ayala's Angel by *Anthony Trollope*   ISBN: *1-59462-352-X* **$29.95**
The two girls were both pretty, but Lucy who was twenty-one who supposed to be simple and comparatively unattractive, whereas Ayala was credited, as her Bombwhat romantic name might show, with poetic charm and a taste for romance. Ayala when her father died was nineteen...   Fiction Pages 484

The American Commonwealth by *James Bryce*   ISBN: *1-59462-286-8* **$34.45**
An interpretation of American democratic political theory. It examines political mechanics and society from the perspective of Scotsman James Bryce   Politics Pages 572

Stories of the Pilgrims by *Margaret P. Pumphrey*   ISBN: *1-59462-116-0* **$17.95**
This book explores pilgrims religious oppression in England as well as their escape to Holland and eventual crossing to America on the Mayflower, and their early days in New England...   History Pages 268

www.bookjungle.com *email: sales@bookjungle.com fax: 630-214-0564 mail: Book Jungle PO Box 2226 Champaign, IL 61825*

QTY

The Fasting Cure *by Sinclair Upton*　　　　　　　　　　ISBN: *1-59462-222-1* **$13.95**
*In the Cosmopolitan Magazine for May, 1910, and in the Contemporary Review (London) for April, 1910, I published an article dealing with my experi-
ences in fasting. I have written a great many magazine articles, but never one which attracted so much attention... New Age/Self Help/Health Pages 164*

Hebrew Astrology *by Sepharial*　　　　　　　　　　　ISBN: *1-59462-308-2* **$13.45**
*In these days of advanced thinking it is a matter of common observation that we have left many of the old landmarks behind and that we are now pressing
forward to greater heights and to a wider horizon than that which represented the mind-content of our progenitors...　　Astrology Pages 144*

Thought Vibration or The Law of Attraction in the Thought World　　ISBN: *1-59462-127-6* **$12.95**
by William Walker Atkinson　　　　　　　　　　　　　　　Psychology/Religion Pages 144

Optimism *by Helen Keller*　　　　　　　　　　　　　ISBN: *1-59462-108-X* **$15.95**
*Helen Keller was blind, deaf, and mute since 19 months old, yet famously learned how to overcome these handicaps, communicate with the world, and
spread her lectures promoting optimism. An inspiring read for everyone...　　Biographies/Inspirational Pages 84*

Sara Crewe *by Frances Burnett*　　　　　　　　　　　ISBN: *1-59462-360-0* **$9.45**
*In the first place, Miss Minchin lived in London. Her home was a large, dull, tall one, in a large, dull square, where all the houses were alike, and all the
sparrows were alike, and where all the door-knockers made the same heavy sound...　　Childrens/Classic Pages 88*

The Autobiography of Benjamin Franklin *by Benjamin Franklin*　　ISBN: *1-59462-135-7* **$24.95**
*The Autobiography of Benjamin Franklin has probably been more extensively read than any other American historical work, and no other book of its kind
has had such ups and downs of fortune. Franklin lived for many years in England, where he was agent...　　Biographies/History Pages 332*

Name	
Email	
Telephone	
Address	
City, State ZIP	

☐ **Credit Card**　　　　　☐ **Check / Money Order**

Credit Card Number	
Expiration Date	
Signature	

*Please Mail to:　Book Jungle
PO Box 2226
Champaign, IL 61825*
or Fax to:　　630-214-0564

ORDERING INFORMATION

web*: www.bookjungle.com*
email*: sales@bookjungle.com*
fax*: 630-214-0564*
mail*: Book Jungle PO Box 2226 Champaign, IL 61825*
or PayPal *to sales@bookjungle.com*

Please contact us for bulk discounts

DIRECT-ORDER TERMS

**20% Discount if You Order
Two or More Books**
Free Domestic Shipping!
Accepted: Master Card, Visa,
Discover, American Express

www.ingramcontent.com/pod-product-compliance
Lightning Source LLC
Chambersburg PA
CBHW081234090426
42738CB00016B/3299